NORWAY 1940-45:
THE RESISTANCE
MOVEMENT

NORWAY 1940—45:
THE RESISTANCE MOVEMENT

BY

OLAV RISTE AND BERIT NÖKLEBY

SECOND EDITION

JOHAN GRUNDT TANUM FORLAG — OSLO 1973

© Olav Riste and Berit Nökleby 1970

ISBN 82-518-0164-8

Front cover: The Home Forces take over from the Wehrmacht at Akershus Castle 11 May 1945.

Printed in Norway by
Petlitz Boktrykkeri As, Oslo
(73-3)

FOREWORD

To those who are familiar with what has already been written by historians about the Norwegian Resistance, this book does not pretend to bring much information that is new. The aim of the authors—both of whom are historians working on related topics—has been to provide a concise survey based on existing studies and aimed at non-Norwegian readers with a serious interest in the subject. To the extent that we have succeeded, most of the credit belongs to the historians on whose original research this survey is based. The book's shortcomings are, of course, our own responsibility.

The authors wish to express their gratitude to the Norwegian Resistance Museum for generous assistance with illustrations.

Olav Riste.   *Berit Nökleby.*

CONTENTS

Foreword

Interregnum 9

Initiatives 14

The Struggle Begins 18

The Fronts are Established 23

A Military Resistance Movement 28

Terror Strikes 33

Watershed 1942 38

    Civilian Resistance 39

    Military Resistance 46

1943: The Long View 56

    New Dimensions 56

    The Heavy Water Sabotage 59

    Looking Ahead 63

    The Activists 67

    New Challenges 70

The Final Year 75

    Milorg: Sabotage and Protection 75

    Civilian Resistance: Preparing for Peace 80

The Liberation 82

Index 92

KIRKENES

TROMSØ

LOFOTEN

NARVIK

BODØ

GLOMFJORD

S W E D E N

MOSJØEN

MAJAVATN

NAMSOS

FOSDALEN

TRONDHEIM

ORKLA

ÅLESUND

ÅNDALSNES

RØROS

VÅGSØY

LILLEHAMMER

BERGEN

RJUKAN

TELAVÅG

DRAMMEN

OSLO

STORD

KONGSBERG

OSCARSBORG

STAVANGER

NOTODDEN

HORTEN

ARENDAL

KRISTIANSAND

The victory of the German forces in Norway, after the two months of fighting which followed the German invasion on 9 April 1940, brought the Norwegian people face to face with tragedy; after 125 years of peaceful existence on the outskirts of world events, the Norwegian nation had in a short span of sixty days experienced invasion, treason, war and defeat. Added to the shock of those events, the future was dark and uncertain. The real masters on Norwegian territory were the German armed forces. In their wake had followed a skeleton occupation apparatus headed, since 24 April, by Joseph Terboven, a former Nazi Gauleiter from the Ruhr district. In the shadow was Quisling, the leader of the small Norwegian Nazi party. To the consternation of the Norwegians and without previous arrangement with the Germans, Quisling had on the evening of 9 April made his way to the microphones of the Norwegian Radio and "deposed" the existing Government, proclaimed his own list of "Ministers" and declared himself Prime Minister. Pushed away six days later, he had since been working for his come-back.

Against this, the continuity of Norwegian sovereignty was embodied in the King and his Government, from the middle of June 1940 in exile in England and all but cut off from contact with their people. Constitutionally their position was strong, and their formal authority to speak on behalf of the nation was generally recognised. Politically, however, it was a government tainted by defeat, and saddled with blame for failing to keep the country out of war and for inadequate leadership during the campaign.

The people of Norway, therefore, were defeated, bewildered and without leadership and guidance. Very few looked to the only authority in the country that could properly be called Norwegian: the Administrative Council, formed in April in

German police troops marching in the streets of the Norwegian capital.

response to the need for a Norwegian civilian authority in the southern and central areas overrun by the German army, a need felt both by Germans and Norwegians and voiced by judges of the Norwegian Supreme Court. The Council's purpose was to keep "the wheels of the nation" turning in the occupied areas and prevent the disruption that seemed certain to result from Quisling's coup.

The terms of reference of the Administrative Council were definitely non-political, however, although the line sometimes was hard to draw. It was also, and particularly from the German point of view, a purely temporary set-up. The Germans' overriding aim in Norway, once their mastery of the territory was complete, was to keep the country calm, in order to draw the expected strategic and economic benefits from Norway without wasting large numbers of troops on a strictly enforced military occupation.

For this aim they wanted the Administrative Council, which

from the beginning had been termed a "government council" in German documents, transformed by degree into an alternative government, supplanting the exiled Government and eliminating the King. They would then conquer this alternative government from within, replacing one by one its present members with men more favourable to practical and political collaboration with the Third Reich. Thus, the Norwegian people would little by little be pushed down the slippery path to satellite status in Hitler's Europe.

In the summer and early autumn of 1940, the Germans, by a shrewd mixture of promises and threats and heavily aided by the success of their armies elsewhere in Europe, came very near to succeeding in their aims in Norway. By the middle of June the Administrative Council was persuaded to meet with the Presidency of the Storting (the Norwegian parliament) in Oslo in order to have a more representative body take part in the decisions which would, in one way or another, determine the relationship between Germany and occupied Norway.

Unfortunately, the parliamentarians had been out of the mainstream of events since, on the evening of 9 April, they had responded to their President Hambro's call for a decree empowering the Government to assume all powers of state until the legislature could again carry out its functions in the normal way. Since then they had been spread throughout the country, subjected to the widespread feeling of hopelessness that was the natural reaction of the man in the street, and the one-sided influence of mass media under German control, without the checks and balances of inside information and daily contact with the political events that were unfolding in Oslo, Berlin, – and London.

In this confused situation, with many of their prominent leaders absent in exile, and impressed by the German threats of imposing a harsh military regime on Norway unless a compromise could be found, the politicians relented on point after point. Having undercut the legal Government since it was absent from the country anyway, they finally, in despair under the immediate impact of France's capitulation, agreed to recommend that the King resign his functions.

11

*7 June 1940: King Haakon enters HMS Devonshire off Tromsö,
bound for Britain.*

Much now depended on King Haakon's reply. To go against
a recommendation from what was after all the most representative body of Norwegians then existing was bound to be an
especially difficult choice for a constitutional monarch of his
strict principles. A rejection of the suggestion would also inevitably expose him to the criticism that it was easy to take a
firm line for those not in Norway and therefore not subjected
to the reprisals and terror that might follow from a refusal to
cooperate with the occupant. Also, what could the King and
the Government offer instead? What could they hold out for
those who resisted Germany's demands on Norway?

It was no easy decision. Yet the King's answer, drafted in
consultation with Foreign Minister Koht, was a sober, solemn
and unequivocal rejection of the suggestion. In the letter,

which he himself read over the BBC transmission to Norway, he stated his conviction that he would betray his constitutional duty to his people if he yielded to suggestions which were necessarily the product of threats and intimidations and not the result of free deliberations. His duty to the Norwegian Constitution, reinforced by the mandate given to him and his Government at the last free meeting of the Storting, was to uphold the nation's sovereignty until such time as the country was again free and normal constitutional processes could be resumed.

Already at the time, this was felt as something of a turning point. The King's answer was rapidly spread by clandestine means all over occupied Norway, printed, duplicated and copied. And although talks to settle the form of regime in Norway continued between Norwegian and German representatives into the early autumn, and a majority of the Storting was willing to suspend the Monarchy for the duration of the war, the talks eventually broke down on the question of the composition of the projected "Council of State" which was to assume the functions of a Government.

After this failure to create a government with at least some semblance of legitimacy and a hope of support from the people, Reichskommissar Terboven had to turn to the minority Norwegian Nazi party, whose leader Quisling and his grey eminence Hagelin had in the meantime been in Berlin canvassing support from German leaders for a renewed takeover bid on their part. On 25 September, Terboven in an angry speech announced the formation of a Council of Commissioner Ministers to run the country "in consultation with", but in fact controlled by, his own German-staffed administrative apparatus, the "Reichskommissariat". The Council was composed of Quisling's men, although the leader himself stayed in the background; Terboven had declared that the road to self-determination for the Norwegian people now went through Quisling's party, which carried the ironic name "Nasjonal Samling" — national unification. Quisling was waiting for that self-determination. Then he would step forward and assume his place at the top.

Reichskommissar Terboven and Police General Rediess, the two leading figures of the German occupation regime in Norway, photographed at an airfield outside Oslo.

The events of 25 September, as will be seen, were tragic in that they ushered in an era of repression in Norway, but at the same time the fog of confusion started to clear. The stakes were becoming visible. The line between collaboration and loyalty could begin to be drawn. The stage was now set for the contest between nazification and resistance which dominated the history of Norway under German occupation.

INITIATIVES

As has already been indicated, the Germans wanted Norway to remain calm and quiet under the occupation regime. Any disturbance, resistance or non-cooperation would diminish the economic and strategic benefits Germany hoped would result from its mastery of the country, and could tie down important forces that were needed elsewhere.

In order to prevent disturbances, it would be necessary to

14

establish and preserve a delicate balance between a stated policy of friendship and cajolery, on the one hand, and on the other a sternly threatening attitude towards any attempt to disturb the calm. Both trends were evident from the start, as can be seen from an episode which occurred on 13 April.

Early in the morning of that day, two young men set off an explosion under Lysaker Bridge which carried the major part of the road traffic between the capital city of Oslo and its airport at Fornebu. The importance of this route for the German reinforcements which were then being rushed into the country was undisputed, and the German military commander in Norway, General Falkenhorst, reacted immediately.

First of all he issued warnings about the serious effects which such acts of sabotage would have, both through punishments for the saboteurs and through reprisals on the population of Norway in general. The first of the later so familiar posters began to appear in the streets, threatening summary executions for the perpetrators of such unlawful acts against the occupant. The deterrent had an immediate effect: on the following day a large group of well-intentioned, prominent citizens published a warning against exposing the civilian population to reprisals by destructive acts like that.

Falkenhorst's second line of action was to lend his support to the efforts of German envoy Bräuer, and others, to replace the odious Quisling "government" by an administrative body more likely to be accepted by the Norwegian people, efforts which culminated in the ceremonial instalment of the Administrative Council.

The "Lysaker Bridge" incident was but an episode. In retrospect, however, it is quite meaningful. First of all it shows that there were people in Norway who were prepared to offer all-out resistance to the invaders, resistance beyond the limits of conventional campaign warfare. But it also confirms that such a resistance was completely alien to the thinking of large segments of the Norwegian population. Finally, the German reaction shows the nervousness of the invader at the prospect of fighting a whole nation instead of a small army.

All these trends were evident through the summer and early

autumn of 1940. German documents demonstrate a meticulous interest in even the slightest sign of anti-German action, combined with uncertainty as to the best way of dealing with it. The Norwegian people, however, remained largely passive. Only a few, inspired in part by the tenacity of certain small pockets of resistance during the campaign, people who fought on regardless of the odds against them, kept the idea of resistance alive. They remembered their Commander-in-Chief's words that "no nation can rise again merely by waiting for something to happen. It must be prepared to help itself as well when the time comes . . ." Hence several of the soldiers hid their weapons and kept in touch with each other. Others began meeting from time to time in small circles of friends, those from sports clubs in particular, anxious to keep together and to keep fit even if they had no clear idea of what purpose would ultimately be served by their association.

At a different level, small, often seemingly childish but sometimes dangerous demonstrations began to occur, directed against Norwegian Nazis and against the German invaders. Posters were torn down, rocks were thrown at German soldiers, Nazi speakers at public meetings were hissed or the meetings boycotted.

The growth of a spirit of resistance during the summer of 1940 owed much to the courage of a few farsighted men. Above all stood King Haakon, whose firm rejection of the call for his abdication dispelled much of the bewilderment and made it easier for Norwegians to decide where to make their stand. But there were others. As the press and radio became increasingly gagged and Nazi propaganda took over, the well-known doctor and public figure Johan Scharffenberg published his clarion call for truth and justice, in protest against the spiritual tyranny which the occupation regime was instituting. "This spiritual tutelage from people not superior in character or intelligence is like slow strangulation. If this is going to be our condition in Norway, then I must again seek comfort in the maxim: vivere non est necesse — to live is no necessity."

Shortly before this, the editor of a local newspaper on the south coast had performed the valuable public service of pub-

16

*For victory with King Haakon VII! These and similar demon-
strations helped to keep the spirit of Resistance alive. In spite
of severe reprisals such symbolic gestures flourished in various
forms—from refusing to sit beside German soldiers on the trams
to wearing paper clips on coat lapels as a sign of "keeping together".*

lishing, on the front page, a complete circular from the occupation regime with revealing instructions on what could and
what could not be printed.

Finally, as a reaction against Terboven's angry and insulting
speech of 25 September, where he implied that the Norwegian
parliamentarians had gone along with the negotiations for a
new "Council of State" for motives of a personal and material-
istic nature, a Stavanger newspaper editor published an in-
cendiary appeal to his countrymen to stand firm in defence of
their democratic heritage, under the heading: "No Norwegian
for sale!"

THE STRUGGLE BEGINS

The effect of the initial skirmishes reviewed above was to prepare the people for the massive attempts at nazification which
followed the institution of the "Commissioner Ministers" on
25 September.

The leading figure in these attempts was the "Commissioner
Minister of the Interior", Quisling's aggressive lieutenant
Hagelin. From many years in voluntary exile as a businessman
in Germany, Hagelin brought with him a strong pro-German
and pro-Nazi attitude and a corresponding lack of understanding for the character of the nation of which he had once been
part.

With the King, the Government and the Parliament elimi-
nated from internal Norwegian affairs, the first target of the
nazification effort was, logically enough, the only remaining
part of the elective democratic process: local self-government.
The formidable strength of the nation's traditions of democracy at the municipal and county level was to be broken up
by the imposition of the "Führer principle", mayors and vice-
mayors appointed by the central authorities and therefore presumably loyal to them, ruling with the aid of an appointed
committee instead of the elected town councils.

The expression "presumably loyal" needs an explanation. In
theory, all the appointments would be made from the ranks of
loyal supporters of the Nazi party. The snag was that there

was not a sufficient number of them to go around. Quisling's party, although it enjoyed a rapid increase in the autumn of 1940 through the influx of opportunists who decided to jump on the bandwagon, still numbered only about 20,000 members out of a population of over three million by the end of the year. Even assuming a high proportion of qualified potential local government officials among them,therefore, the ambitious nazification programme would have been difficult to carry out. As it were, quite a number of those appointed were loyal Norwegians who had previously held municipal office.

For these men, however, their appointment posed a difficult moral problem. If they rejected the offer, such a refusal to co-operate, while exposing them to the danger of reprisals from the Nazi authorities, would be an evident patriotic gesture. But would not the wider consequence be to clear the path for the appointment of persons who would be neither willing nor able to protect legitimate Norwegian interests?

On the other hand, a patriotic Norwegian who continued to serve as a town official under the new regime might possibly be able to influence, soften or sabotage the "new order" and thus promote more permanent Norwegian interests, if he was willing to take the risk.

This dilemma was in fact basic to the whole resistance. The range of choices ran from uncompromising, all-out resistance to each and every attempt to enforce the occupation regime, to more of a "business as usual" attitude, leading to a considerable degree of practical cooperation for the purpose of keeping the wheels turning and avoiding disruption and chaos in the country's economic and social life. Somewhere each individual had to draw the line, and social pressure, police terror and legal complications meant that there was no really easy way out for those who had their country's best interests at heart. The choice was most difficult at the beginning: later, as the fronts became clarified and the issues presented themselves in a more naked form, the range of alternatives was progressively limited. But the dilemma never totally disappeared as long as the occupation lasted.

The Nazi penetration of local government was only partially

successful. In the school committees, for example, the percentage of Nazi members in the spring of 1942 ranged from 0 in the county of Sogn og Fjordane to 58 in the region of the capital. In the nation as a whole only every fifth committeeman was a member of the Nazi party. In the municipal councils, the "new order" was more widely established. However, not all the new officials were willing tools of the Nazi regime, and some of the appointed mayors were able, for a time, to alleviate the impact on their towns of the "new order". But most of those who did attempt any really effective sabotage of the dictates from above were soon replaced, making it increasingly difficult for those who remained to justify their continued service.

The fact that it came at such an early stage, and that the persons involved were individuals scattered all over the country with no common organisation or other means of contact and consultation with each other, gave the take-over bid for local government only a limited effect on the construction of a united resistance front. In this respect, the assault on the country's judicial system had a much more momentous impact.

The Supreme Court, as the only pillar of the Norwegian constitutional system still functioning, was from the first moment determined to stand for the principles of justice. Their opportunity came when the "Commissioner Minister of Justice", Riisnæs, in November 1940 attempted to abrogate the independence of the courts of justice by giving himself the sole right to appoint or dismiss jury members, assessors and persons with related judicial functions.

In a sharp letter, the Supreme Court denounced this attempt as a breach of the Hague Convention relating to the rights of occupation, of the fundamental constitutional guarantee of independence of the courts, and of the laws governing the composition and procedure of the courts of justice. Riisnaes angrily counter-attacked by changing the laws concerning retirement from public office, so that officials who were within five years of the normal retiring age could only remain in office at the mercy of the minister concerned. This measure, which would enable the Minister to achieve control of the Supreme Court by stacking it with loyal followers of the new regime, was ac-

The empty Chamber of the Norwegian Supreme Court, as it appeared after the Judges resigned in protest against the unlawful measures of the occupation regime.

companied by a letter from Reichskommissar Terboven denying the right of the Supreme Court to test the validity of orders issued on his authority.

The reply of the Supreme Court came in December. In a letter to the Minister and to the Reichskommissar the Court took a clear stand in defence of the Constitution and laws of Norway, and the basic principle of the independence of the courts of justice. The refusal of the occupation authorities to respect those principles, the judges concluded, made it impossible for them to remain in their posts.

The veneration in which the Supreme Court was held by most Norwegians gave the resignation of its judges a tremendous effect. It also served as an indication of the futility of attempts at accommodating or cooperating on the practical level with the new regime, thus helping to draw a clearer line between resistance on one side, and collaboration and fellow-travelling on the other.

Much of the bewilderment and confusion which had been so prevalent among the Norwegians in the summer of 1940 was therefore dispelled by the end of the year. The nazification assault on national institutions and democratic processes, and the clumsy way in which it had been done, stiffened the opposition to the "new order". The heavy-handed reaction of Quisling's followers to any kind of demonstration or patriotic gesture merely increased the number of persons taking a clear stand against the regime.

Even more important, links of communication began to be forged between individual resisters and between resistance groups. Underground tracts, brochures and newsletters began to appear and to be circulated from hand to hand, providing information which the censored newspapers could not bring, and giving guidance on how to meet each new challenge from the regime.

No less important was the guidance, leadership and inspiration reaching occupied Norway from England. The Norwegian service from the BBC in London, instituted just after the German invasion, provided a vital corrective to the biased picture emerging from the nazi-controlled news media. Radio speeches by the King and—as the crisis of confidence in their leadership created by the successful German invasion began to wear off—by members of the exiled Government, began to create links of national unity in the new struggle against Nazi oppression.

But words were not sufficient. Already before the campaign in Norway had ended, the forerunner of the British Special Operations Executive had initiated clandestine operations against the Germans in Norway, and had recruited their first Norwegian agents. The arrival of an increasing number of Norwegian volunteers in the British Isles, escaping from Norway in fishing vessels, even in rowing boats, enabled the Government in London to start preparing for an active Norwegian contribution to the Allied struggle, and the only prospect for immediate action aiming at the liberation of Norway was in clandestine operations. Just a few weeks after the Germans seized control over the whole of Norway, two radio stations were in operation in the country, transmitting information about German naval movements to the British Intelligence Services. And by early autumn, ferried across the North Sea in fishing vessels, the first agents were sent for the purpose of establishing contact between the Government and the resistance groups being formed in Norway. For a long time yet, communication was haphazard and faulty, but a beginning had been made.

THE FRONTS ARE ESTABLISHED

The outcome of the struggle during the autumn of 1940 about the democratic structure of Norwegian society — government, parliament, judiciary and local government — was more of a defeat than a victory for the forces of nazification. Their second line of attack in this ideological war of aggression was directed towards gaining control over the minds and convictions of the people. This contest brought into focus two separate institutions: the Church, and the schools.

Normally, the Church and the schools in Norway are the responsibility of a separate government department, the Ministry of Church and Education. An overwhelming majority of the people are members of the Lutheran State Church, and education is largely public—state or municipal, but under uniform national control. Through the "Commissioner Minister of Church and Education", therefore, the NS possessed the basis for an attempt to enrol religion on the side of the "new order" and also, more ominously, to indoctrinate nazi ideology into youth and children on the pattern so successfully followed in Germany.

The first skirmish in this spiritual struggle is all the more remarkable in that the Church took the initiative before that institution had become the target for directly repressive measures from the authorities. At the end of October 1940, the leaders of religious organisations combined to declare their faith in Christian unity and their determination to defend the tenets of their beliefs. The significance of the declaration lay not so much in its contents, which were purposely apolitical, but in the fact that it laid the foundation for a common front, of representatives of high church, low church and other Lutheran groups which had so often been torn by bitter factional strife. To give formal expression to this significant unity, they

23

formed the "Joint Christian Council of the Norwegian Church".

The strength of this united front became apparent soon after New Year 1941, in a series of declarations combined in a "pastoral letter" which was spread all over the country and read from many pulpits. Taking issue with the increasing instances of violence by Quisling's uniformed "hird" units, the leaders of the church broadened this to a demand for respect towards the principles of justice, and freedom of conscience, upon which a Christian nation was built; "When state authorities permit violence and injustice and exert pressure on human souls, then the Church becomes the guardian of consciences. One human soul means more than the whole world. The bishops of the Church have therefore laid on the Ministry's table some of the facts and official proclamations of recent times concerning the nation's public affairs which the Church finds contrary to the law of God ... Consciences are troubled in our parishes now, and we feel it our duty to give to the men of the State a clear expression of the voice of the Church."

The conflict between the teachers and the authorities began as the result of a more direct provocation, as in November 1940 it was learnt that each teacher was to be asked to sign an individual declaration of loyalty to the new regime, expressing his or her willingness to "work positively and actively to promote my pupils' understanding of the new ideology and view of society as stated in the programme of 'Nasjonal Samling', and for the actions and decisions of our new national government". Forestalling this action on the part of the Ministry, the teachers' organisations provided their members with a standard formula of reply. Instead of loyalty to the regime, this proclaimed a willingness to "remain faithful to my teacher's calling and my conscience, and on this basis to follow, now as before, the directives for my work justly given by my superiors". As a result, the Ministry's efforts for the time had to be abandoned.

These impressive demonstrations of solidarity in opposition to the nazification attempts of the "new order", and of faith

24

Quisling speaks.

in the principle of freedom of conscience, meant another major step towards a clarification of the issues raised by the occupation. It was becoming increasingly difficult to remain uncommitted; fence-sitting was no longer comfortable; day by day people had to choose sides and become involved.

The real drama of civil resistance in this early stage, however, was the outcome of the new regime's attempt to harness the country's large voluntary organisations for the cause. Modern society, as we know, is a veritable cobweb of voluntary associations, whether professional, trade, charitable, social or sports organisations and societies. And in many cases the citizen looks more toward his association to promote his special interest, rather than to the government which exists to advance the common good.

Basing themselves in part on the fascist doctrine of the corporate state, which regarded the parliamentary system of representation as outmoded and wanted instead a congress composed of spokesmen of professional, trade and other economic interest associations, the Norwegian Nazi authorities began planning a system whereby the NS party could control these associations and in that way exert pressure on the members.

The initial, persuasive rather than coercive, effort took place in the autumn of 1940, and was directed against the trade organisations of farmers and fishermen. In the political confusion that reigned in the early autumn, the party succeeded in working out with representatives of the farmers a plan for a new "Norwegian Farmers' Organisation" which would declare its adherence to the "new order". By the time the plan came up for final ratification by the old farmers' associations, however, the climate of opinion had changed sufficiently to deprive the Nazi authorities of their expected victory. In the similar case of the fishermen's associations, clear-sighted representatives managed to delay the plans in the eminently sensible conviction that time was on their side and not on that of the NS party.

That time worked for the opponents of the "new order" was clearly demonstrated in the case of the sports associations. Here the impatient and heavy-handed "Commissioner Minister of Sport" soon got tired of the efforts at persuasion, and simply ordered a "Norwegian Sports Association" to be set up under the Ministry's supervision with compulsory membership. The reaction was overwhelming: a national "sports strike" which lasted for the duration of the war and was practically 100 per cent effective. All patriotic competitors and spectators boycotted public sports events, with the devastating result of reducing national championship competitions to third-rate contests with only a handful of spectators.

By the end of 1940, the negotiation phase of the regime's efforts to subvert the organisations had resulted in total failure. Neither farmers, fishermen, nor any of the several associations of medical and health personnel that had been wooed, had concluded an agreement with the authorities. And during the winter and spring of 1941, while the regime prepared more severe measures, the organisations not only resisted but counterattacked. Active resistants in various national associations made contact with each other for the purpose of coordinating their actions; when the Ministry of the Interior proclaimed regulations aimed at ensuring political conformity in the civil service, 22 large organisations of civil servants and connected occupations issued a common letter of protest on 3 April 1941 to Reichskommissar Terboven.

If the protesters had expected a change in the regime's policies, they were disappointed. But the effect of the letter, a copy of which had been promptly dispatched to London and read on the BBC's Norwegian service before it had reached the Reichskommissar, was a new demonstration of anti-Nazi solidarity which served to widen the scope of the organisations' next step: a letter of protest dated 15 May and signed by representatives of 43 leading associations. The main purpose this time was to promote by an openly political action the creation of a united Resistance front of the widest possible range. It was no longer only a question of the integrity of the civil service, but of justice under the law for all Norwegians, against "proclamations and decisions openly contrary to international law, Norwegian law and Norwegian sense of justice in general . .

[measures] which materially violate the protection of personal safety afforded by our laws."

A reaction was this time inevitable. On 12 June the Gestapo interrogated and arrested three of the signatories; and on 18 June the leaders of the 43 organisations, surrounded by armed police, were addressed at a meeting in the parliament building by the Reichskommissar himself. After his scornful and menacing speech, six more signatories were arrested. The "Commissioner Minister of the Interior", Hagelin, thereafter proclaimed the dissolution of several associations and the appointment of party commissioners for others. The notable exception of the trade unions was easy to understand: the Germans had no desire for a disruption of the nation's economy which could damage their war effort.

In many respects, the events of 18 June mark the end of the "open" phase of Resistance. Through mass resignations of members and officials, organisations like the Norwegian Medical Association, and the associations of dentists, engineers and lawyers, vanished from the surface, leaving empty shells behind. But they continued to exist underground, developing with time into a vast invisible framework of organised civilian resistance under tested leaders, issuing guidance and directives in liaison with the national Government in London. Lacking experience in clandestine work, coordination — among different organisation committees, between civilian and military Resistance leaders, and with London — was both dangerous and difficult. Nevertheless, by the beginning of 1942 a "Coordination Committee" had been formed for some of the organisations which had been forced under ground, to function as a secret general staff in the war against nazification.

A MILITARY RESISTANCE MOVEMENT

As mentioned above, the first courier sent out by Norwegian authorities in London landed in Norway in September 1940. His report, after a stay of several months, pin-pointed the many difficulties that had to be overcome before a coordinated movement could be established. Although he found much evidence that the willingness to resist was strong, there was a need for leadership and guidance at every level, local, regional and national, to tell people what to do, and how to do it. Above all they needed communication with London. The radio transmitter which the courier brought over from England was woefully inadequate, and the report gives a telling account of the long hours spent in attempts to achieve contact with the original equipment, and then in efforts to re-build the set.

Before a resistance movement can be built up, some basic requirements need to be fulfilled. First of all, a widespread underground movement can hardly exist without at least the passive support of a majority of the population at large. Next, it needs access to sources of positive outside support, providing arms, equipment, money, instructors, and overall guidance. We have already seen how the spirit of resistance was being fostered and spread by the events of 1940/41 in Norway, pointing towards the fulfilment of the first of these fundamental requirements.

In the matter of access, Norway was exceptionally fortunate among the occupied countries in that both the border to neutral Sweden and the jagged North Sea coastline were too long to be effectively closed by the Germans. Contact with Britain, though increasingly hazardous, remained open, and in the summer of 1940, London was the scene of several important initiatives, on the British as well as on the Norwegian side.

"To set Europe ablaze" was the colourful purpose of a strange organisation set up by Churchill in July 1940 and named "Special Operations Executive". In more factual terms, its task was to organise, assist and direct Resistance movements in enemy-occupied territories in conjunction with the overall Allied war effort. It was an organisation without precedent, and regarded by many with scepticism if not with suspicion. Those who believed in it, however, saw the possibilities of a three-fold contribution from that kind of activity: it would keep up and strengthen Allied morale while wearing down the spirit of the occupation forces; it would be a useful tool of economic warfare through sabotage activities; and it could be-

A Norwegian fishing smack in the rough waters of the North Sea. Some never made it across to Shetland: the heaviest loss was the "Blia" which disappeared with 42 people in a storm in November 1941.

come a valuable fifth column behind enemy lines during Allied offensive operations.

In September 1940, seven Norwegians were already under training by SOE as agents. Among them was lieutenant, former actor, Martin Linge, who soon became the leader and the prime spirit of Norwegian assistance to SOE. In time this contingent grew into "Norwegian Independent Company No. 1", better known as "Company Linge".

Before the end of 1940, SOE's efforts aimed at Norway had made some headway. In addition to the agents being trained in Britain, an SOE section was in existence at the British Legation in Stockholm, and the nucleus of a fleet of fishing boats for transport across the North Sea was established in the Shetlands. A few contacts had been formed with occupied Norway, and occasional sabotage actions had been carried out, with no significant result. In a document dated 11 December 1940, SOE had formulated its "Norwegian policy", an optimistic and spirited plan for a nation-wide guerilla organisation to be kept in readiness for a future Allied invasion, coupled with a programme of sabotage and propaganda activities to be carried out by special agents from Britain. Largely for reasons of security, control would be kept strictly in British hands.

By the end of January 1941, SOE had established its first wireless station in Norway. The operator, who had landed on the coast from a submarine, was also organising resistance groups around his base near the southernmost point of the country. The Allied programme of direct action in Norway, however, began with a raid organised by the Directorate of Combined Operations for which SOE provided specialist personnel and assisted in the planning. This was "Claymore", a hit-and-run operation against the Lofoten Islands in North Norway on 4 March 1941, which destroyed a number of processing plants for fish products in the area and brought back to Britain a number of Norwegian volunteers as well as German and NS prisoners. Later that spring another smaller but similar raid was carried out by the Norwegian navy.

Parallel to this, but independent of SOE, Norwegians in occupied territory were slowly trying to build up their own secret military organisation, which by the late spring of 1941 had the discernible contours of five regional "fighting groups" and a sentral leadership. But the groupings were loose, and internal coordination was limited. Contacts with the Norwegian authorities in Britain and with SOE were restricted to occasional messages brought out through Sweden or across the North Sea, along one of the many escape routes organised by special "export groups" and used both by couriers, by fugitives from the Gestapo, and by youths wishing to enlist in the Norwegian forces abroad. As the summer of 1941 approached, the leaders of the military organisation in Norway consciously adopted a cautious policy. Living in the country, they felt the increasing watchfulness of the German police and the repression and the arrests that occurred, particularly in the wake of the Allied raids. The conflicting approaches of SOE and Milorg (or military organisation in Norway) came to a head in a curious incident later in the summer.

In an effort to reach an understanding with the Norwegian

31

Government in London, the leadership of Milorg on 10 June wrote a letter characteristically addressed to the King, in which they set out the plans and purposes of their activities. Briefly their aim was to prepare cadres for a secret army which, when the time was ripe, would be activated and armed for action in conjunction with an Allied invasion. The letter explicitly warned against sabotage actions in the meantime, and expressed no desire for arms at that time.

The letter was sent by courier to a liaison officer on Shetland, but was then held back since it was felt that it gave an incomplete picture of the organisation in Norway and raised supplementary questions. A copy reached the SOE, however, whose Scandinavian Section replied with a directive on the lines of SOE policy without formal consultation with Norwegian authorities.

The British reply was a clear call for action in Norway. It stressed the importance of Norwegian territory as a possible target for large-scale Allied landings, and urged the creation of an armed and trained secret army, ready to assist in such operations. In the meantime, carefully planned sabotage actions should be carried out, both for reasons of economic warfare and in order to compel the German army to hold large forces in Norway. Above all, the directive emphasised the need for close coordination of the Norwegian Resistance with Allied military plans and operations. This contrasted with the assertion of the Milorg letter that they would be under the orders of an internal leadership whose authority was to be recognised by the King.

This reference to an internal leadership was the source of much confusion and misunderstanding, and arose from the peculiar difficulties of working underground, without proper communications. Contrary to Milorg's belief, a leadership of that nature did not exist, and the Norwegian Government, when informed of the contents of the Milorg letter, took it to be a rejection of the constitutional authorities in favour of a rival government inside Norway.

Fortunately, the need felt on both sides of the North Sea for contact, understanding and coordination was about to be met.

In the field of civilian Resistance, several men who had played a role in the struggle against nazification decided to send a representative to London. He was welcomed by the Government and appointed to a Cabinet post in September 1941. Two months later, after consultation with two Milorg leaders who had come to London to try to sort out the misunderstanding surrounding the exchange of letters referred to above, the King and the Government officially and formally recognised the Military Organisation as a branch of the Norwegian armed forces. The Milorg council was placed directly under the Army High Command. From 1942, when the armed services were joined together in a Defence High Command, Milorg's affairs were dealt with through a special bureau of that Command. By that time, however, it was a new and different Milorg.

TERROR STRIKES

At the beginning of September 1941, the first wave of Nazi terror was building up in Norway. Among its main ingredients were Terboven's continuing struggle with Norwegian organisations, Germany's attack on the Soviet Union,—and a modest quantity of milk.

We have already seen how the Reichskommissar's desire to get at the Norwegian trade unions was tempered by the economic necessity of extracting the maximum benefit from the Norwegian economy for the German war effort. The German attack on Russia in June stressed this dilemma even further. For this all-out assault on "the evils of Bolshevism" a tight control of the trade unions became an imperative necessity. And not only the trade unions: the war against Russia meant that Norway moved much closer to the centre of strategic concern, in which no sabotage or other disturbance could be tolerated. A rule of fear would have to be substituted for the rule of pressure and threats.

The trigger that released the terror was a spontaneous strike among workers in Oslo against the cessation of deliveries of special milk rations to workers in factories. Coming after the progressive worsening of the food situation over a long period, this measure must have seemed like the straw that broke the camel's back. Meat, butter and eggs had all but disappeared from the diet in Norwegian cities, real coffee was a thing of the past,—even potatoes were scarce at times. And now milk was to go the same way.

The strike was unofficial, and the trade union leaders, warned by the Germans that it would have the most dangerous consequences, vainly tried to prevent the walk-outs. In the evening of 9 September the fury of the strikers was subsiding, and the metal workers voted to return to work the next morning. But the Germans had now decided to act. Early the next morning a state of emergency was declared, and the Gestapo went into action. With the streets of the capital guarded by armed police, a wave of arrests took place, concentrated against the trade unionists. That same evening, the first list of sentences was announced by the head of the German Sicherheitspolizei in Norway. Two young trade union leaders were condemned to death for incitement to strike, whereas in fact they had done their utmost to hinder it; the two death sentences had already been carried out by an execution platoon in the hills north of the city.

For six days Terboven's hatred swept the city. Then, with the lesson of terror thus brought forcibly home, the state of emergency was lifted. But arrests, executions, torture and prison camps had come to stay. Through the rest of the year, whole networks of emerging Resistance groups learnt the cruel lesson of security and caution as the police, sometimes guided by informers and infiltrators, struck at their leaders. These arrests, together with those shot for "collaboration with the enemy" and for espionage before the September state of emergency, and the many who had to go abroad to escape from the Gestapo, meant a veritable decimation of the pioneer leadership of the Resistance by the end of the year. And the reconstruction, whether of military groupings, intelligence networks, or "export groups" to organise the escape of Norwegians to Sweden or the British Isles, was a slow, dangerous and often discouraging job.

34

Grini prisoners on parade. This prison camp on the outskirts of Oslo was the largest in the country. To many of its inmates, however, it was only a forewarning of the horrors of the concentration camps in Germany.

One of the measures instituted by the Germans in connection with the September state of emergency was the requisitioning of all wireless sets. This action amounted to a tacit admission that the occupation authorities, with their controlled broadcasting and the censored press, were losing out in the contest for the minds of the people. The decision cannot have been taken lightly, since it meant not only switching off the powerful and authoritative voice of the BBC and its Norwegian service; it also meant that the "new order" had given up any hope of influencing the people through their own broadcasting. Presumably, therefore, the authorities already considered this a lost cause.

The most important result of the decision to requisition the radios was the flourishing growth of an underground press.

A secret listening post, receiving the latest news from London for distribution through "illegal" newspapers. Newspapers work was highly dangerous and brought heavy casualties, since the people had to "expose" themselves in order to spread their products.

From its modest beginnings a year earlier, this activity now grew into a veritable industy, which in its heyday was to count over three hundred different newspapers and kept thousands of people busy. Some papers appeared regularly, others irregularly, and many died an abrupt death, as the highly dangerous work of distributing the products as widely as possible took its toll. But the value of these "illegal" newspapers, with titles such as "Whispering Times" or "London Radio", their contents sometimes concealed inside such innocent wrappers as "Potato-growing in your garden", can hardly be over-estimated. Besides offering a welcome antidote to the heavy-handed Nazi

36

propaganda, they provided the links in the growing barrier of patriotic solidarity. For as individuals, the Norwegians were hardly by nature any more "heroic" or staunch anti-Nazi than any other nation, but with the courage and leadership of the few, and the means by which they could reach the many, a unity was created whose strength withstood the test.

As the winter of 1941—42 approached, there did not seem to be much light at the end of the tunnel. At home, the people faced increasing shortages of food and supplies in addition to the mounting severity of the occupation regime. Abroad, although the attack on Russia meant that Britain no longer stood alone among the great powers in defying the German war machine, the penetration of the German army deep into Soviet territory made it doubtful whether the Russians could hold on through the winter. When, despite this, the spirit of Resistance was not broken, the explanation must be sought in the experiences of the preceding twelve months—in the gradual hardening of the will to resist produced by the alternating interaction of Nazi challenge and patriotic response. Although the probing of the occupation authorities had found some soft spots through which they could penetrate, the most notorious one being the widespread willingness to accept employment in the construction of airfields, military camps and fortifications, they achieved no real break-through.

Even after giving due credit to foresighted Resistance leaders, we can now see that the Nazi regime contributed to its own defeat by its tactics. We have described how Terboven's original idea aimed at pushing the Norwegians inch by inch down the slippery slope of collaboration. It might have worked. But clumsiness and impatience created the necessary environment in which Resistance could grow and gain strength. Germany's alternative, of course, would have been to deliver a stunning blow of terror and reprisals right from the start, nipping every effort to resist in the bud. But the eight-week campaign following the invasion, and after that the attempts, for ideological reasons, to win a Nordic nation by cajolery and then through a sympathetic movement of fellow travellers, ruled out any consideration of that alternative. Hence the Germans and their

37

Norwegian assistants in a sense got the worst of both worlds: first, by giving patriotic Norwegians time to be "persuaded", they in fact gave them time to recover from the initial blows and to prepare the ground for an anti-Nazi front. Then, when terror and violence really hit, the front had grown sufficiently strong to react to it as a challenge rather than as a deadening blow.

WATERSHED 1942

For the Resistance the year 1942 was to be both tragic and triumphant. Tragic because of the terror and the loss of lives; triumphant because the NS attempt at nazification met such vehement resistance that by autumn 1942 Quisling had actually lost any chance of ever being given real power over Norway by the Germans.

The fight against nazification was indeed a "people's struggle", with very broad participation. An important secret behind this rallying of the nation against Quisling is found in the fact that skilful and foresighted leaders on all levels guided their less politically minded countrymen. Another factor was the merciless ostracizing of those who failed to act as "good Norwegians", which proved a very successful way indeed of keeping weaker persons within the ranks. The so-called "ice front" meant that "traitors" were socially isolated; friends, neighbours, even family, kept their distance; their children were frozen out by their comrades. This rather harsh treatment was, however, effected not so much by way of punishment for those already on the other side, but as a warning for those who might be tempted to follow suit. Thus the ice front prevented pessimists from taking a step they would undoubtedly have deeply regretted afterwards.

The central civilian Resistance leadership as it existed in Oslo by the end of 1942 consisted mainly of two groups, which were cooperating; in fact, several of the leaders were members of both groups. The first one, called the Circle (Kretsen), counted, among others, former members of the Supreme Court and the Administrative Council, as well as prominent labour

Chief Justice of the Norwegian Supreme Court, Paal Berg. A man whose advice was sought more than offered, his prudence and balanced judgement gradually thrust him to the forefront as the undisputed over-all leader of the Norwegian Resistance Movement. (See also p. 78.)

leaders. It made its first appearance in the summer of 1941, but did not function on a continuous basis until a year later. The Circle's main task was to keep contact with the Norwegian Government in London. In close cooperation with the other group, it gradually was to take over the leadership of the civilian Resistance. The Coordination Committee (KK) was formed after the professional organisations had been forced under ground during the clash with Terboven in the summer of 1941. The group was started in October 1941 to act as an executive for the organisations in their continued but now clandestine struggle, and was fairly well organised by the beginning of 1942—just in time for its first hard test.

Civilian Resistance

At this stage of the war civilian Resistance was mainly directed against NS. In the course of the year matters reached a climax, because Quisling now set out to show that he was master of

39

the situation. In the contest that followed the Germans mainly stood aloof; Terboven had been told to let Quisling alone. He obeyed orders, and furthermore he had no objection to standing aside and watching the Norwegian Nazi leader destroy himself.

Having been kept in the background behind the "Council of Commissioner Ministers" since September 1940, Quisling had spent over a year hoping for better times. But a sort of promise from Hitler at the beginning of December 1941 had made Quisling believe that 1942 would see his real take-over in Norway. A few weeks later, however, the war situation had changed for Germany. The U.S.A. had declared war on Germany; the Russian offensive had put the Germans in a difficult and perhaps critical position on the eastern front; and two new British raids on the Norwegian coast (Lofoten and Vågsøy) had strengthened Hitlers' strong conviction that the awaited Allied invasion would take place in Norway. It was therefore imperative that the Norwegians should keep calm; Hitler wanted no trouble in Norway.

Thus the "Machtübernahme" or take-over bid that Quisling carefully staged at the old fortress Akershus in Oslo on 1 February 1942 was nothing but a comedy. Despite the pompous ceremony installing him as "Ministerpresident", Quisling and his "government" had little real power. The Germans were still in firm control. But nevertheless NS got a freer hand to nazify the nation. The Quislings saw a way to power through this nazification; if successful, they would have shown that they had mastered the situation and could eventually be entrusted with the governing of Norway.

They therefore set out to indoctrinate the youth, to dominate school and church, and to force the professional organisations to form a corporative "Riksting", a kind of occupational and professional National Assembly to ensure Nazi dominance over them. On all these fields NS met fierce resistance. The leaders of the civilian Resistance clearly saw the danger of the Quisling scheme; if the front broke down here, it was highly doubtful whether the Nazi advance could ever be stopped.

On 5 February Quisling's new government passed laws that

Vidkun Quisling, accompanied by Terboven and Rediess, arrives at Akershus Castle for the pompous ceremony installing him as "Ministerpresident".

established a national youth organisation on the model of the German "Hitlerjugend", and a Nazi teachers' association with compulsory membership for all school teachers. Both laws met immediate protests.

The national youth organisation, the NSUF, was created to indoctrinate youth with Nazi ideology. Every boy and girl between 10 and 18 years had to attend. In the weeks to come, the Ministry of Church and Education received masses of protests. The Church of Norway immediately objected. A secret instruction distributed to parents resulted in more than 200,000 letters to the Ministry, in which parents under full name and address told the Nazis that they would not have their

41

children participate in the NSUF. The teachers joined in this chorus, the fight for the youth becoming an integral part of their own fight for the freedom of the schools.

The struggle over the schools was to be a bitter one. On 15 February the leaders of the teachers' Resistance urged all the teachers to protest openly against the NSUF and against compulsory membership in the Nazi teachers' association. The result was overwhelming: some 12,000 of the 14,000 teachers in Norway protested. Then the Ministry tried to force them to withdraw their protests: those who did not, would lose their jobs by 1 March. Practically no one gave in. This put NS in an embarrassing position, as the Nazis had publicly boasted that only a few teachers opposed the new law. If they were to dismiss all those who had really objected, practically no school would have teachers after 1 March.

As a temporary way out the Ministry declared a month's holiday, starting on 27 February, "because of the fuel situation". This could not, however, solve the problem for Quisling. The contest had reached a deadlock. It is highly probable that Terboven had watched Quisling's efforts with a certain glee—he was not dismayed by the fact that the new Ministerpresident had made a fool of himself. But now matters had gone too far; he could not allow the Resistance to win a really crushing victory over a government which the Germans themselves had set up. He therefore intervened in the fight with the teachers.

On 20 March 1942 1,100 teachers from all over the country were arrested and sent to concentration camps. An additional 200 were arrested during the next couple of weeks, but in spite of rough treatment and threats only a handful gave in and joined the association.

Terboven's next move was to send 500 of the arrested teachers on a nightmarish voyage on board a small coastal steamer, originally certified for 150 passengers and now packed with 500 prisoners in addition to 50 German guards. The 1,600-mile voyage northwards along the coast from Trondheim started on 15 April. Despite ominous rumours that the Germans intended to sink the ship en route, it nevertheless reached Kirkenes on 28 April.

42

Norwegian teachers at Kirkenes, as seen by one of them.

Now some dreadful months followed for the school teachers. They were put to hard labour, in spite of terrible living conditions. The housing was inadequate, to say the least; sanitary conditions beyond description; and the food and drinking water at times a direct threat to their health.

In August the sick were allowed to go home, on condition that they joined the association and took up teaching when they got home. After some discussion the teachers then decided that a winter in Kirkenes under such conditions would endanger the lives not only of the sick, and there was no point in any more sacrifice at this stage; the struggle of the teachers against NS had in fact already been won. The NSUF had come to nothing, likewise Quisling's plan to use the new teachers' association as a part of his "Riksting". The front among those teachers who had not been arrested also held. On 25 April 1942 the Ministry of Education had declared that the law concerning the new association had been "misunderstood", the association was not intended to be *political,* and the idea that the teachers would be obliged to participate in the work of the NSUF was a "complete misunderstanding". The teachers had won their battle.

Quisling also found himself in open conflict with the Church. NS interfered with church rights and tried to use it for Nazi purposes. It was soon clear to the bishops that they could not continue under Nazi domination, and on 24 February 1942 the Ministry of Church and Education received letters from all the bishops declaring that they were resigning from office in protest against the NS violation of church rights. They would, however, continue their work outside the State Church. The clergy declared itself loyal to the bishops, and in most churches all over the country a declaration was read on 5 April, making the stand of the Church clear to the nation.

Quisling answered by having several church leaders arrested, but he had actually lost the fight: of the 699 clergymen of the Church of Norway, 645 resigned, and 151 out of 155 ordained priests serving in various capacities outside the Church followed suit. Quisling was left with a "State Church" without a clergy. He tried to remedy the sad fact by ordaining priests with rather doubtful moral and educational background. In fact, the Church continued its work throughout the war, but separated from the state. Whereas the Nazi clergy preached to empty churches, services held by the dismissed clergy were overcrowded, in some degree because people had a need for religion in those trying times, but also because it was a way to demonstrate against Quisling and NS.

Thus by April 1942 Quisling had managed to raise a determined front against him; he was in open fight with the teachers, the clergy and the parents. Terboven, who was responsible for keeping Norway quiet, therefore stopped another of Quisling's plans before it could be carried out. This plan would have meant compulsory membership for workers and employers alike in a new organisation which was to replace the existing trade unions and employers' associations. But, as the Reichskommissar commented, if the workers should go on strike too, he would have the whole nation in rebellion.

The final test for civilian Resistance in 1942 came when Quisling tried to establish a new form of national assembly, "Riksting", a corporate body replacing an elected parliament in which all the professional organisations should be repre-

A vicar of the "New Order" celebrates Sunday service with a congregation of one in a West Coast village church.

sented. Wisely enough he had not mentioned this plan to the Germans.

In August 1942 the Ministry of the Interior in utter secrecy began to prepare for the summoning of a "Riksting". The Resistance movement managed to get hold of these plans and immediately started a counterattack. Instruction was sent to the members of all the organisations to withdraw their membership. To stop this, NS passed a law that made membership of an organisation compulsory for people of certain professions. This only had the effect that the instruction to withdraw was repeated, and this time the members were also to protest against the new law.

Again the demonstration against Quisling was overwhelming. In some of the organisations up to 100 % withdrew, and a similar instruction to the trade unionists resulted in an estimated number of at least 100,000 withdrawals. But Hitler had now lost his patience with Quisling. Instead of gaining control over the nation, the Ministerpresident had managed to arouse the greater part of the Norwegian people in open fight against him. Quisling was told that the Führer wanted no discussions about Norway's future before the war was over. Furthermore, any contact with Berlin would have to be made through the Reichskommissar. Hitler would have no direct approach from Quisling any more; Terboven alone was responsible for civilian affairs in Norway.

The fight against nazification had ended with triumph for the civilian Resistance. NS was never again allowed to launch similar schemes. The front against Quisling and NS had hardened, and the larger part of the nation had been made aware of the value and importance of civilian Resistance. Last, but not least, the apparatus of Resistance leadership had proved successful. Communication between central and local leadership had been good, and the system of guiding people by means of instructions had been tested and found utterly effective. It had been a difficult and trying year, but through it civilian Resistance had come of age.

Military Resistance

Whereas civilian Resistance during 1942 mainly fought the NS, military Resistance intended to play a part in the warfare proper, and its role must be viewed on a world war background. In spite of what his military experts said, Hitler was quite sure that the Allied invasion would come in Norway. The British raids on the Norwegian coast in December 1941

46

Fortress Norway—German coastal batteries on guard against an invasion that never came.

made him even more certain of this, and in the course of 1942 he therefore pushed through a massive military buildup in order to turn Norway into a veritable fortress, Festung Norwegen. The number of Wehrmacht soldiers rose from 100,000 at the end of January to about 250,000 in June. By the autumn of 1942 the Germans were well prepared to meet an invasion in Norway.

There were actually plans for an Allied attack in Norway in 1942. Stalin was pressing for a second front, and Churchill favoured an Allied invasion in North Norway. However, his "Operation Jupiter" was never carried out; instead the Allies attacked in Africa, "Operation Torch", in November 1942.

There was considerable secret military activity in Norway in 1942. The British organisations SOE and Secret Intelligence Service (SIS) both sent agents to work in the field; and the home organisation, Milorg, was also organising with a view to playing its part. But the notion that the invasion was imminent stimulated a premature growth of the secret military groups in various parts of the country. One still does not know for certain the source of this optimism, although many Norwegians had expected the British to "come back" all the time since June 1940. Another factor may have been careless talk from agents and other leaders. There was a tendency to underestimate the need for security precautions, because it was thought that time was short. The Germans being on the alert and the invasion not coming, it is easy to see now that the result had to be a catastrophe. The costs were to be high for military Resistance in 1942.

The agents sent in by SOE and SIS were all Norwegians, but trained by the British. SIS was not involved in any activity of the home organisations; its sole interest was military intelligence from Norway, and its agents had strict orders to avoid unnecessary contact with people at home. These agents worked in utter secrecy, and little is known and less written about them. Their task was to establish radio contact with the U.K. for the transmission of intelligence to the Allies. In 1942 the main interest of the British was to get reliable information about the German navy. A greater part of the German battleships, among them "Tirpitz" and "Scharnhorst", had been sent to Norway, partly in connection with Hitler's preparation against invasion and partly to cut off the convoy route by which Allied war material was being sent to North Russia. About 16 SIS radio stations, situated along the coast from Oslo to Tromsø, sent invaluable naval intelligence, giving the allied navies a day-to-day picture of the German naval positions.

The SOE men all belonged to Company Linge, one of the most highly decorated Allied units in World War II. In 1942 they carried out 21 operations, from sabotage to missions to help create a secret army in Norway. The number of men in each party varied from one to ten or fifteen. Most of the Linge men were sent in by sea; the fishing vessels, whose frequent crossings earned them the name of the "Shetland Bus", brought in 49 of them during the sailing season 1941/42, but this year

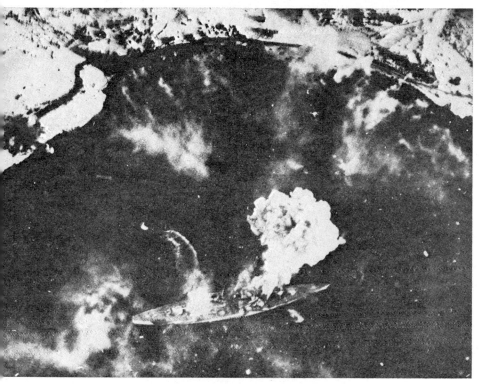

Aerial photo of the German battleship "Tirpitz" in a fjord in North Norway after a bombing attack.

also saw the first Linge parachute jumps, 21 of the agents com ing in by air.

The majority of the parties was engaged in instructing local groups, and, wireless contact between the U.K. and Norway being of vital importance for effective work, most of the expeditions included radio operators. Thirteen SOE radio stations had contact with the Home Station in England in 1942.

SOE, suspicious of the ability of the Norwegians to form effective secret military organisations, had forbidden its agents to seek contact with Milorg. This policy was still pursued in 1942, but was changed in the course of the year. The Linge men found it impossible and indeed dangerous to create new military groups where a home organisation already existed. They therefore soon began to cooperate with Milorg.

During 1942 cooperation and unity of purpose was also gradually established at the top level, between the British and the Norwegian military authorities in London. In matters concerning military Resistance in Norway the control was in the hands of the Norwegian section of SOE and a special department of the recently established Norwegian High Command. In February these two formed the Anglo-Norwegian Collaboration Committee (ANCC). SOE had at this time still not quite overcome its suspicions regarding Milorg and their policies still differed, but the existence of the ANCC contributed much to improving the relationship at all levels.

Milorg was nearly paralysed at the beginning of 1942, after the severe blows inflicted on it by the Gestapo the previous autumn. As a result the central leadership in Oslo had all but lost contact with the district organisations. By February/March, however, the networks began to be repaired and a re-organised Milorg slowly gathered strength again.

The re-organisation implied among other things a strengthening of the central leadership, which gradually became an effective leadership for a country-wide organisation. The process had of course to be a slow one, but during the year Milorg took the shape that it kept, with minor changes, throughout the war. Locally, the former five districts were replaced by fourteen smaller units. Milorg counted by now several thousand men, but it was to a large extent an army without weapons. The number of men under arms can only be surmised but a total number of two to four thousand has been estimated.

At a meeting in Stockholm in February 1942 between representatives from Milorg and the Norwegian High Command, the policy of the former was defined. Milorg should be prepared to give aid in case of an invasion, but until this aid was needed the organisation should take care not to expose itself. As for weapons from the U.K., Milorg wanted nothing except what was necessary for instruction.

In spite of this careful policy, 1942 was to be a year of exposure and catastrophe for military Resistance as a whole. The

German vengeance in all its thoroughness: The village of Tela-vaag is razed to the ground.

Gestapo in Norway did its best to fulfil the promise given by Goebbels in spring 1942, commenting on the stubborn Norwegians: "If they won't learn to love us, they shall at least learn to fear us!" The first actions of the Gestapo against the military Resistance in 1942 cost 20 Norwegian lives. With the help of the infamous informer Henry Oliver Rinnan, the Germans succeeded in infiltrating an "export" group in Ålesund, on the west coast. This group cooperated with Milorg and other secret organisations, sending refugees and volunteers for the Norwegian forces across the North Sea in fishing vessels.

A boat with 23 people on board was taken by the Gestapo just as it was ready to sail for Shetland on 23 February 1942. All on board were arrested, and another 20 arrests followed shortly. One of the arrested men was executed a few days afterwards; another was shot during reprisals in Trondheim later that year; and 18 young men were shot as a reprisal because two Gestapo officers had been killed in a fight with SOE agents in the small fishing village of Telavaag near Bergen.

The Telavaag area was an important transit centre both for SOE and SIS. Both organisations sent agents and equipment to this district and picked up their men there after their missions had been completed. It was inevitable that the inhabitants of

51

Telavaag would know that something was going on. The disaster came when a woman, jealous because she found she had not received her share of the coffee and other things brought in by the agents, told the Norwegian Nazi sheriff about her grievances. Then a man bragged about what he had seen in the house of the local merchant—weapons, ammunition, radio sets—and the policeman knew enough to act. He warned the Gestapo in Bergen, who arrived by boat early in the morning of 26 April 1942 and went directly to the merchant's house.

Unfortunately two Linge men were staying there at that time; both were radio operators, on their way to Stavanger and the Oslo district respectively. In the gun fight that followed, one of the agents and two Gestapo officers were killed; the other agent was wounded and taken prisoner.

The Germans took a terrible revenge. The wounded agent and the 18 young men from the boat in Aalesund were executed. Telavaag was wiped out; all the houses, more than 300, were destroyed. The cattle were killed or taken away, and all the fishing vessels were sunk. The entire male population, 76 men between 16 og 65 years old, were deported to concentration camps in Germany, where most of them died. The rest of the inhabitants, 260 persons, were interned in Norway.

More was to come. At the end of May two other Linge men, who had established a radio station near Bergen, were surprised by the Gestapo. The Germans had come on their track when a Norwegian "too honest to lie" had shown them where to find an arms dump. The two agents were arrested, tortured and then shot. In the wake of these tragedies further arrests followed all over western Norway. Many of those who managed to avoid being arrested had to leave the country, and the result was that for the rest of the year the military Resistance groups in that part of the country were more or less paralysed.

As in the west, the reversals of military Resistance in eastern Norway started with the arrest of a Linge agent. He had been acting as an instructor to Milorg groups in the district and was arrested at the beginning of May. After a couple of months this arrest was followed by numerous arrests among Milorg leaders in Oslo, Drammen, Kongsberg, Horten, Notodden and other places. At the same time, the end of July, an SOE radio operator, who had established his station on the eastern side of the Oslofjord, was captured by the Gestapo; the Milorg district leader and several other Milorg men were subsequently arrested. As a result of all the arrests on both sides of the fjord, military Resistance work in eastern Norway came almost to a standstill by summer 1942.

In the west and east the reason for the Gestapo's success is probably to be found in the interaction between carelessness and unfortunate circumstances. It is impossible to avoid all risk in clandestine work, and no secret organisation can guard itself entirely against leakages. Nor should the antagonist, the Gestapo, be underestimated. It was a highly effective police organisation, spurred to extreme vigilance by the fact that the Führer wanted no trouble in Norway.

In the north, however, it seems that special circumstances brought on the tragedy. The events must be viewed in connection with the British plan "Jupiter", the prospective invasion of northern Norway. As part of the preparations for a landing, SOE sent in three operational groups during winter 1941/42. The Linge men were to build up a military organisation in the district around Mosjøen, approximately half way between Trondheim and Bodø. This guerilla force should be ready to "cut Norway in half" in the case of an invasion further north. They should have no connection with Milorg, which by the way was practically non-existent in that part of the country.

From December 1941 till July 1942 large numbers of the male population in the district were busily and eagerly engaged in transporting, on their backs, tons and tons of arms and ammunition. In retrospect, it is easy to see that this could not last; such an activity could not be kept secret for a very long time. On 6 September the Gestapo struck. Acting once more on information from Rinnan and his men, the Gestapo arrested the radio operator. To rescue him his comrades opened fire when he was forced to show the enemy an arms dump near the lake of Majavatn; two Germans were killed, but all Linge men managed to escape.

During this period also, a British combined operation to destroy an electric power plant at Glomfjord, and thereafter an SOE sabotage operation on the iron ore mines at Fosdalen, were carried out; Terboven was alarmed at these signs of Allied military activity in this strategically important district, and decided to set an example.

A state of emergency was declared in the whole area from Majavatn in the north to Røros in the south, including Trondheim, and lasting from 6—12 October. A number of arrests took place, and 34 Norwegians were executed, 10 of them as mere reprisals, while the others belonged to the military organisation and had been arrested after the Majavatn affair. These tragic events were to make the work of military Resistance in this area practically impossible for some time.

In the north it seems to have been the amount of arms and ammunition brought in—more than 24 tons in all, and the intensive building up of an organisation, that contributed most to the strong belief that an invasion would take place in the immediate future. The authorities in London may not have made any mention of actual invasion plans. But it is only too human to believe what one deeply wants to believe,—and this also helps to explain the similar expectations which influenced the secret organisation work in the southernmost part of Norway. Although the British had no plans for an invasion there at the time, optimism was as strong as in the north, and the result as tragic.

SOE had several agents in the district arround Kristiansand, but Milorg had the largest military organisation. At first there were frictions and rivalry between the Linge men and the local groups, but this was overcome during the year and Milorg got valuable help from the specially trained agents. By the summer of 1942 Milorg in this district counted an estimated 5—600 men. Their arms were those which had been hidden away early in the war; what SOE sent in was destined for its own agents.

Milorg prepared for invasion. As it was thought that time was short, one had to work fast—too fast. The rapid growth of Milorg made it very vulnerable. The invasion did not come,

A Milorg group undergoing secret training in the forests "some-where in Norway".

and time worked for the Gestapo, which by December 1942 knew enough to act. What followed was to be one of Milorg's most serious set-backs. A number of the leading men were arrested, and many others had to leave the country, leaving a nearly paralysed district organisation. Total loss of lives amounted to more than 50 when the Gestapo investigation was at last over, one of the casualties being the district leader himself, who was executed with 5 of his men.

The losses suffered by military Resistance in the tragic year 1942 had been a hard lesson. The district organisations as well as the central leadership had to start afresh. It was now acknowledged by all the parties involved, SOE, the Norwegian High Command, and Milorg, that cooperation between them was essential. There was no room for competition, and from now on military Resistance in Norway worked more carefully, with a long-term policy. It was becoming clear that the liberation of Norway would not come till the war had been won on other fronts. Until then the secret military groups would have to "lie low and go slow"", so as to avoid confrontation with the enemy before the time was ripe.

1943: THE LONG VIEW

New Dimensions

Until 1943, the Resistance in Norway had been confined to limited perspectives. Internally the struggle had chiefly been one where the nation had tried to find itself in response to the challenge of nazification. Nazification had failed: the forces standing for loyalty to the King, the Government and the ideals they represented, had proved the strongest.

At the same time, the military elements of the Resistance had been labouring under the pressure of narrow time limits, imposed from outside by desires for spectacular exploits which would stimulate Allied morale, and inspired on all sides by the belief that the Allied invasion of Norway was in the making.

From 1943 all this was to change. The ideological defeat of Nazism in Norway was a means as well as an end in itself. The patient who has fought off a dangerous and insidious virus attack cannot rest on his laurels: during the struggle he has become vulnerable to other infections. Therefore, after a short period of retrenchment and consolidation, strength must be built up and increased in order to resist even stronger attacks in the future.

What in fact seemed to be about to happen in Norway, as 1942 drew to a close, was that, while the ideological contamination had been rejected and Norway's soul so to speak had been saved, the body had increasingly been drawn into the German orbit in the service of the Axis war economy. Although Norwegians might spend their free time looking forward to the Allied victory, quite a number of them spent their working hours in activities which in various ways benefitted the German war effort.

56

Bekanntmachung

Durch das Krie... ...nd am 20 Oktober 1943 wegen Verbrechen gegen die Verordnung zum Schutze der besetzten norwegischen Gebiete vom 12. Oktober 1942 folgende norwegische Staatsangehörige verurteilt worden :

A) Wegen Betätigung für einen Feindstaat und Unterstützung von Agenten

Johan Jörgensen-Rotvaag	35 Jahre alt, wohnhaft in Rotvaag	
Johan Hammer	33 Jahre alt, wohnhaft in Aarviksand	
Haakon Kristiansen	27 Jahre alt, wohnhaft in Aarviksand	
Edelsten Johansen	22 Jahre alt, wohnhaft in Nordre-Rekvik	
Helmer Albrigtsen	24 Jahre alt, wohnhaft in Nordre-Rekvik	

zum Tode

B) Wegen Betätigung für einen Feindstaat :

Ottar Jörgensen   19 Jahre alt, wohnhaft in Aarviksand

zum Tode

C) Wegen Unterstützung von Agenten :

Öivind Larsen   47 Jahre alt, wohnhaft in Tromsdalen
Otto Jörgensen   66 Jahre alt, wohnhaft in Rotvaag

zum Tode

Petra Jörgensen   46 Jahre alt, wohnhaft in Aarviksand
Astrid Hammer   23 Jahre alt, wohnhaft in Aarviksand
Dagny Jörgensen   28 Jahre alt, wohnhaft in Rotvaag

zu 15 Jahren Zuchthaus

D) Wegen Nichtanzeige des Aufenthaltsortes von Agenten :

Sigurd Jörgensen   22 Jahre alt, wohnhaft in Aarviksand
Karl Lauritzen   32 Jahre alt, wohnhaft in Nordre-Rekvik
Karl Jörgensen   55 Jahre alt, wohnhaft in Aarviksand
Simon Albrigtsen   50 Jahre alt, wohnhaft in Nordre-Rekvik
Haakon Kristiansen   44 Jahre alt, wohnhaft in Nordre-Rekvik

zu 15 Jahren Zuchthaus

Elvin Jörgensen   64 Jahre alt, wohnhaft in Aarviksand
Freidian Andersen   31 Jahre alt, wohnhaft in Aarviksand
Ingvald Johansen   24 Jahre alt, wohnhaft in Nordre-Rekvik

zu 12 Jahren Zuchthaus

Einar Jörgensen   30 Jahre alt, wohnhaft in Aarviksand
Bernhard Jörgensen   62 Jahre alt, wohnhaft in Aarviksand

zu 10 Jahren Zuchthaus

Otto Olsen   55 Jahre alt, wohnhaft in Tromsö

zu 6 Jahren Zuchthaus

Das Vermögen aller Verurteilten ist eingezogen. Die Todesstrafen sind vollstreckt

22 Oktober 1943.   Der Gerichtsherr

"... The property of those sentenced has been requisitioned. The death sentences have been carried out."

Some of these various ways were clearly to be condemned. Those who with few or no reservations produced goods for the Germans, or who offered their services in the construction of barracks, airfields and other facilities for the German forces, could rightly be accused of assisting the enemy. And many of them were, in the postwar trials. In all, over three thousand sentences were passed for profiteering, and another five thousand were sentenced for having volunteered for work on German installations. Even so, these figures hardly convey an adequate impression of the lamentable willingness of many Norwegians to take the inflated wages offered for work which served German interests.

To many others, however, the question of what work you should do offered a real dilemma. Short of letting the economy come to a standstill, where should the line be drawn between a level of economic activity that kept the nation alive and healthy, and economic assistance to the enemy? Take for instance fish oil, the only available raw material for margarine in Norway during the war, and therefore a vital contribution to the population's diet since butter soon became only a memory. A by-product of fish oil is glycerine, very useful for the manufacture of ammunition. Do you let the people go without their main source of fat, or do you let the Germans get their glycerine?

These and similar dilemmas did not and do not lend themselves to easy solutions, but by the beginning of 1943 the problem was at least being faced and the search for solutions had begun. With the hope of an early end to the war being replaced by more long-term planning, economic warfare became more important. In their search for more supplies of all kinds, the Germans further tightened the screws of economic exploitation in every occupied country. Moreover, as Hitler never wavered in his conviction that an Allied invasion of Norway was being prepared, fortress Norway was continually being strengthened with more forces and new defence installations. The forces had to be fed, and more labour was needed for construction.

Also, now more than ever, the Germans had to be on their guard against any disturbance of their economic exploitation, or any other Resistance activity that was likely to facilitate an Allied invasion. In this way also, the pressure on Norway was increasing. In London attention with regard to Norway was being shifted from spectacular pin-prick raids and preparations for an early Allied invasion to economic warfare and plans for the final liberation of all of occupied Europe. So far, the main weapon against the Axis economy had been bombing, and bombing was also tried in Norway. From the autumn of 1941 several bombing raids had been carried out against Norwegian fish oil factories, with mixed results, as has already been suggested. When the Norwegian Government realised that several important Norwegian industrial plants were on future target lists, they together with SOE suggested sabotage as a less costly and more accurate alternative. The airforces were not altogether convinced of the argument. Proof in action was needed.

The Heavy Water Sabotage

In the evening of 27 February 1943, nine uniformed Norwegians climbed down an ice-covered precipice near Rjukan, crossed a small river, and crawled up the equally steep other side of the valley, to a heavily guarded industrial plant on the mountain side. The armed German guards taken care of, some of the men entered the factory and placed their explosive charges in carefully selected spots. After midnight a muffled explosion echoed through the narrow valley; an ardous, long-prepared venture had been crowned with success, 500 kilogrammes of heavy water had been destroyed, together with several vital parts of the production plant. Why all this fuss for a load of water which, although it was called "heavy", looked and felt and tasted like most ordinary drinking water?

The answer lies in the chemical formula deuterium oxide, a special kind of water which was a vital ingredient for the method chosen by the Germans in their efforts to win the race for the ultimate weapon of mass destruction: the atomic bomb. Knowing this, and knowing that the plants of Norsk Hydro near Rjukan in southern Norway were the Germans' only source of this fluid, the highest Allied authorities in early 1942 had made this plant the Number One target in Norway. The Norwegian section of SOE and specialists in the Norwegian High Command now went to work, and before Easter 1942 the first Norwegian agent was on the spot. More than half a year later he was joined by four men from Company Linge, and together they prepared to receive two glider plane loads of British Royal Engineers who were to carry out the actual sabotage operation. They never met. Because of bad weather one glider became detached from its tug plane and crash-landed. Those who survived the crash had no reason to praise their luck: they were killed by the Germans. The other plane with its glider in tow crashed against a mountain, and no one survived.

Operation "Freshman", the code name for the glider attempt, alerted the Germans that an attack on the heavy water plant was being prepared, and they increased their vigilance in the area. Meanwhile, the reception group carried on in their mountain hut despite the cold and the lack of food, until a group of six men from their company was dropped by parachute into the area in the middle of February 1943. The rest of the operation went without a hitch. And despite the 3,000-man search mounted by the Germans to comb the whole area and make arrests by the dozen, five of the saboteurs skied 250 miles in full uniform to the safety of Swedish territory, two went to Oslo to work with the military organisation, and four remained in the area.

For two of the men who were left in the mountains, the heavy water was to present another challenge. After finding out that the production of heavy water had been resumed, the Combined Chiefs of Staff ordered a bombing raid on the plant in November 1943. The raid was not very successful, and twenty-one Norwegian lives were lost in the attack. As the Germans nevertheless decided to move the heavy water stocks and the production machinery to Germany, the two men still in the area consulted London and it was decided to attack the ferry which would carry the heavy water supply accross a lake. This final stage of the heavy water sabotage occurred on 20 February 1944, as explosive charges sent the ferry to the bot-

Towards the end more and more men and supplies arrived by parachute drop. This picture is from the mountains near Trondheim.

tom of the lake. Unfortunately fourteen Norwegian civilians went with it.

The attack on the heavy water was not the only sabotage action carried out in Norway during 1943. Other successful operations were mounted against the pyrites mines of Orkla, which provided the Germans with important supplies of sulphur. Another action, against silicon carbide works near Arendal, interrupted production for several months. And there were several others. However, many operations either could not be carried out, or did not produce the desired results. Sabotage was proving more difficult than SOE had thought. On the other hand, the bombing raids, mounted at greater cost, were not proving much more successful. In fact, the most successful industrial attack was carried out as a Combined Operations raid against the pyrites mines at Stord outside Bergen, when a Norwegian-British force landed from motor torpedo boats and

Industrial sabotage: An aluminium factory south of Oslo, which made sheet metal for German airplanes, has been visited by six masked men.

wrecked the plant so thoroughly that it took two and a half years to bring production back to a third of normal capacity.

A number of other sabotage actions carried out at other times during the war by Norwegian agents sent from Britain, assisted by Milorg men, did not appreciably alter the general conclusion, that sabotage as a weapon of economic warfare had a strictly limited effect. A few factories had their production interrupted for some time, and a number of ships were put out of action, but on the whole, apart from the special case of the heavy water where the object was not economic but essentially military, Germany's economic exploitation of Norway was not seriously hampered. However, the sabotage did force the Germans to spend much time, money and effort in protecting the industries and installations in order to avoid any disruption of their war economy. And, to the other side, each sabotage action which was carried out, even though harsh reprisals might follow, helped morale and stimulated faith in the ultimate victory of the Allies. In 1943 this was perhaps needed more

The German transport ship "Donau" aground in Oslofjord, wrecked by a magnetic "limpet" mine placed by saboteurs of the "Oslo gang".

than ever. After more than two and a half years of occupation, deprivation and reprisals, many were becoming war-weary, and the end was not yet in sight.

Looking ahead

Still, planning and organising for the liberation went forward, despite many problems that had to be overcome. It was becoming increasingly clear that Norway would only regain its freedom as part of the final liberation of all occupied Europe. But even then, several alternatives were possible. The strong German forces in Norway might refuse to capitulate, even after the German armies on the Continent had laid down their arms. In that case, the Allied armies would have to fight their way into the country, and Milorg would presumably have an active part to play in assisting the invading forces. Another possibility was that the Germans might decide to evacuate Norway in order to concentrate their armies in the defence of their central positions in Europe. Massive measures would then have to be prepared to prevent economic and political chaos. Finally, in case of total and simultaneous German surrender on all fronts, an orderly take-over would have to be assured, and large German forces would have to be taken care of.

In all these cases, the role of the Resistance would be crucial, particularly that of Milorg and the clandestine police organisation. In order to prepare the Resistance for these tasks, the fullest understanding between the Resistance and the Government in London was absolutely necessary. Only in that manner could the Resistance act with the necessary authority and take power on behalf of the Government during the transition. In the meantime, the military elements of the Resistance would have to be supplied with arms and equipment, and instructed in the various tasks they would have to perform. Or should they? Would not an insufficiently armed, equipped and trained military movement merely be offering itself for slaughter by the powerful German army, either before or during the liberation of the country? And would not the discovery of a secret and extensive military network in Norway offer the Germans the excuse they waited for in order to start a massive campaign of reprisals and terror, thus bending the will to resist beyond the breaking point? These were points in debate during 1943, both inside the Resistance and between the Resistance and the Government in London.

The debate started off with a memorandum from the Norwegian Defence High Command in London to the Council of Milorg at home, on the subject of enemy reprisals. The purpose was to get the Council's advice on a fundamental dilemma: was it best to attempt to bring forward the date of the liberation and the end of the distress of occupation by an agressive Resistance policy? Or would the sum of the population's suffering be less if a passive attitude were adopted, even if the liberation would thereby be postponed? The Defence High Command had for its part tried to steer a middle course, avoiding un-

A Milorg man on guard duty "somewhere in Norway".

necessary loss of life through reprisals, but not letting the fear of reprisals alone hinder a policy of active Resistance.

The Milorg Council's reply, in January 1943, made it clear that Milorg envisaged, and wanted to prepare for, a strong and effective effort of assistance to an invasion of Norway, and was ready to face the increased reprisals which would be the result. The Council had no doubt that this readiness was shared by the majority of the population, and stressed the national value of an active Norwegian Resistance: it was important for the future "that the people may find strength and self-respect in the knowledge that the liberation was not only a gift from others but also a result of their own efforts". Milorg therefore wanted supplies and clear directives to enable them to carry out their tasks in connection with the liberation. The emphasis on assisting an Allied invasion, however, would make it necessary to be careful about actions in the meantime, in order to keep the organisation intact for the final effort.

Before sending their reply to London, the Milorg Council had consulted with what they thought to be the overall leadership of the Resistance. In the meantime, however, the "Circle" had established themselves as a kind of "inner Cabinet" of the Resistance, and they got hold of the document. Their reaction, no doubt influenced to some extent by the fact that the people of Milorg were unknown to them and therefore regarded with suspicion, was a firm rejection of such a policy.An eventual struggle between the well-trained German forces and inexperienced young Norwegians led by amateurs could only result in what they called a "children's crusade" of no military use. Moreover, the population would not support such activities, and had no preparation for or experience of the mass terror and reprisals that would be the result. As to the national importance and moral value of a Norwegian rising, the "Circle" saw the non-violent struggle as the real Norwegian contribution to the defeat of Nazism. In unity and discipline in the face of provocation lay the strength of the Norwegian nation.

This internal dispute was eventually resolved when the civilian and military Resistance leaders could meet and begin to clear up the misunderstandings. In the meantime, the basis for a closer contact and understanding between Milorg and the Norwegian High Command had been made at a meeting in Sweden in May 1943. It was then settled that the main guide-line for future military Resistance work in Norway would be to prepare, train and arm units for assistance to an Allied army of liberation, and for the maintenance of law and order after a German surrender in Norway. This meant a strict subordination of Milorg to Allied command and strategy, and was accompanied by a tightening of the reins by which the various Milorg districts were controlled by the central Milorg leadership in Oslo. Until then the authorities in London had tended to regard a central leadership inside the country as an unnecessary and dangerous element of interference. The new policy therefore represented a strong vote of confidence in the forceful new Milorg leader, who led the re-organisation process after the setbacks of 1942, and who was to lead the Home Forces for the rest of the war. He was Jens Christian Hauge, lawyer, age 28. This confidence was soon to be shared by the civilian leaders, and during the autumn a joint programme was agreed.

The official policy was set out in a document which in itself was an impressive manifestation of the unity of the Home Front: dated 15 November 1943, it was submitted jointly by the Milorg Council, the leaders of the clandestine police organisation, and the civilian leadership. This document stated that the aim of Milorg was to establish a military preparedness at home which the Norwegian High Command could use for purposes in connection with the re-conquest of Norway.

The activists

The danger of such a policy, with its restrictions against actions by Milorg before the liberation, was that more activist-minded groups might decide to break out and act on their own. We have seen earlier how the British, through SOE, had gone in for a more active policy in Norway than that advocated by Milorg. That dispute had by the spring of 1943 become a thing of the past, especially since Norway was no longer in the front-line as a possible target for an early Allied invasion. But the desire for action was still strong in many quarters in Norway, and the cautious official line on sabotage and guerilla warfare had already for some time been under attack from the left.

From the time of the German attack on Russia the Norwegian communists, although few in number, had made a certain impact on the Norwegian scene. Tightly organised, active, disciplined and with a certain flair for conspiratorial activities, they tended to keep to themselves, although occasional contacts occurred between them and the other Resistance organisations. Efforts at coordination usually failed, for two reasons: mutual suspicion, and a fundamental disagreement on aims and means between the policy of moderation advocated by the central leadership and the far more activist course of the communists. The activism of the communists may have had several explanations: a genuine conviction that only an all-out struggle could provide a significant contribution to the defeat of the Germans, coupled with less regard for the sanctity of human lives including their own; a desire to become the vanguard of Norwegian Resistance, and thus establish their claim to a larger role in post-war Norway; or instructions from Moscow.

In any case, their active sabotage policy was noticeable in Norway already in 1942, although it is still in many cases difficult to determine whether this or that spectacular act of sabotage was carried out by communist organisations or by independent activist groups. At the time, every sabotage not officially sanctioned by London and Milorg was usually referred to as irresponsible, for obvious reasons: whatever policy was determined for the Norwegian Resistance, it was vital to ensure that it was adhered to by all. In-fighting and anarchy could easily reach such an extent as to assist rather than hinder the enemy, with disastrous results. Today it is possible to take a less jaundiced view, and to recognise that although some sabotage is irresponsible one can also err on the side of caution; the officially determined middle way was not necessarily always the right choice. But the reasons advocated for the cautious official line were the result of careful analysis of the situation, and had a persuasive ring: "We are convinced", the letter of 15 November 1943 said with regard to a policy of active assault on the enemy, "that it will bring disasters to the people and the country which will be out of all proportion to the military gains, and that it will disrupt and destroy the longer-range

Since not enough arms could be supplied from abroad, Milorg began manufacturing their own. Here home-made Stenguns are being test-fired.

work of civil and military preparations which promise to be of the greatest importance to the nation." And there was yet another reason. The Norwegian people, according to the Resistance leadership, had not been prepared to withstand the pressure of really large-scale terror and reprisals which would follow any offensive from the Resistance.

There were times in 1943 and 1944 when the Resistance leaders seriously feared that the strict moderation imposed on their ranks might cause impatient or activist sections to break away. This helps to explain why the leaders of Milorg early in 1944 began to demand a more active role for their organisation, a demand which was only to some extent granted in the directive issued after the Normandy invasion. But the "official" Resistance had one powerful argument against an activist break-out: the control of the supplies of weapons and equipment from Britain. Besides, they and only they were recognised and approved by the Norwegian High Command, the Government, and the King. The importance of this fact was further strengthened when Crown Prince Olav in the summer of 1944 assumed the position of Commander-in-Chief of all the Norwegian armed forces, including the forces of the military Resistance organisation.

New Challenges

Although it was stated earlier in this chapter that the German pressure on Norway was increasing during 1943, this needs some important qualifications. First of all, it should be noted that the occupation regime in Norway was mild compared with the conditions prevailing in East Europe and in some other European countries. Terror, mass arrests, torture and murder were used in Norway, and to the victims it was scant comfort to know that they were comparatively few on a national scale. But characterised as a whole, Norway suffered far less than most other occupied countries. To some extent this was because Norwegians had the dubious honour of being regarded by the Nazis as a kindred people, a misled Nordic tribe that should preferably be led into the fold of the millennium through persuasion.

By 1943 the ideological offensive had bogged down. Thereafter there was less need for German restraint in the treatment of the Norwegian population, and, although this did not result in a regime of mass terror on the scale known in other countries, the Germans were on their guard against an intensification of Resistance activities. Thus, after an activist sabotage group attacked a German military train in the Drammen area in October 1943, five men were quickly executed in reprisal. This again prompted several thousand well-meaning and peace-loving citizens to publish a condemnation of such dangerous sabotage activities—an indirect confirmation that large numbers of the population were not hardened for war and terror.

In August 1943, eleven hundred Norwegian officers were arrested and sent to Germany. The Germans did not like the idea of their presence in Norway, where they might be useful to the Resistance or to the Allies in the event of the invasion

Oslo's University Square 13 November 1943: The students are being arrested.

which the Germans still feared. Later that autumn a fire in the University Hall in Oslo gave Reichskommissar Terboven a long awaited opportunity to vent his hatred of the intellectuals. Over a thousand male students and several professors were arrested two days later, the University was closed down and seven hundred students were sent to a special camp in Germany for "indoctrination".

The main challenge to Norway in this period, however, was the so-called "Total National Labour Effort". In spite of the willingness of many Norwegians to take employment with the Germans, and the import of thousands of slave labourers from Russia and East Europe to work on grandiose construction projects in North Norway, the shortage of labour in Norway was becoming more serious. On 22 February 1943, a vast propaganda campaign heralded the new labour effort: all able-bodied Norwegians were to be registered, allegedly to create a labour reserve which could be used to increase the Norwegian food production. The Resistance leadership at first acted cautiously and hesitantly. More food might not be such a bad thing. So when the real purpose of the registration turned out to be to provide a labour reserve for German military installations, some damage had already been done. The target figures set by the Germans were never reached, but this owed much to the incompetence of those set to administer the effort; this administrative confusion was again in no small measure due to a successful Communist coup in which one of the "labour effort" offices was blown up and the registration cards scattered to the winds.

During attempts to prevent sabotage against the "labour effort", Quisling's fury in August 1943 centred on the Norwegian police. All through the war the Norwegian police were in a difficult position. They were pressed to join NS, and even those who managed to resist had to obey orders that were contrary to their conscience. On the other hand, a "good Norwegian" could, as a policeman, give invaluable help to Resistance organisations and people in danger. Thus one day in the autumn of 1942 many of the Jews remaining in Oslo were warned by policemen that something was likely to happen shortly. Unfortunately, the warning either came at too short notice or went unheeded for other reasons, because the following morning most of the Jews were arrested and deported to Germany—and the Norwegian police had to make the arrests.

Undoubtedly the regime was aware that it could not trust the Norwegian police, and, after a police officer in early August 1943 refused to arrest young girls for evading compulsory labour service, Quisling proclaimed a law putting the police under military law, and had the police officer executed. On 16 August some 470 policemen of all ranks all over the country were arrested, and 271 of them were sent to a concentration camp near Danzig.

In the autumn of 1943, Quisling, in another attempt to prove that Norway under his leadership was a worthy and valuable ally of Germany, conceived the idea of mobilising 50,000 Norwegians for war service on the Eastern Front against Russia: in his efforts to recruit volunteers for such service, begun in 1941, he had not managed to muster more than about 2,000 Front Fighters. The German officer on the Reichskommissar's staff to whom the mobilisation order came treated it with scorn. The mobilisation of 50,000 would require an equal number of trusted men to ensure that those drafted did not escape to Sweden.

The idea was brought up again in the first weeks of January 1944, this time by Quisling's aggressive and widely feared "Minister of Justice", Riisnaes. He had close relations with the German SS leaders, and suggested the call-up of 75,000 Norwegians aged 18—25 for service with the SS troops on the Eastern Front. Riisnaes had fewer illusions about the willingness of Norwegians to serve, and suggested a series of precautionary measures: the Swedish border and the coastline would have to be sealed off to prevent a mass exodus of Norwegian youths, and those who did not report for enrolment at short notice would immediately be brought in by German policemen or soldiers. They would then have to be shipped to Germany as soon as possible—still unarmed—and dispersed into many different SS units for service against Russia only. Then, but only then, was Riisnaes prepared to trust them.

Fortunately, a courageous woman in the Ministry of Justice realised the importance of the letter, copied it, and managed to pass the copy to the Resistance leadership. An initial doubt about the authenticity of the copy was solved by sending an agent on a nightly visit to Riisnaes' office, where he broke into the safe, "borrowed" the original letter, and showed it to the Resistance leaders. By next morning the letter had been returned to its place in the safe. This time the leadership decided to act at once, not to wait and then react after the mobilisation had begun. Through all available channels, including the Norwegian transmissions from London, firm warnings were issued against anybody following orders from the authorities to report for "labour service". The already established "labour service" was considered the most likely machinery for the first stages of the mobilisation. At the same time a series of sabotage actions was carried out against the offices and registration centres of the "labour service". Evidently, anyone who was told to

"Present Spades!" Quisling reviews a labor service unit on parade.

report and did not show up was taking a grave personal risk. The authorities had made this quite clear. Even so, about thirty per cent stayed away in the first round of registration. In May 1944, the intelligence network of the Resistance understood that the second round was about to begin, and during a hectic week instructions were sent out that nobody should report for the so-called "national labour effort". The effect of the warning this time was wholly convincing: not only did very few report for registration, but thousands wisely took the precaution of disappearing into the countryside, the forests or the mountains.

Later in the summer, the regime tried to play its last card in this particular contest. In the forthcoming issue of new ration cards—and few things were not rationed by this time—the cards for those who had not reported for labour duty would be withheld. To the Resistance leadership, which already had a very difficult supply situation to cope with, this could have been a serious blow, and quick action was needed. Thus, when a lorry full of new ration cards was on its way one August morning through the streets of Oslo, it was hijacked by a gang of saboteurs and taken into a nearby backyard where the precious cargo was transferred to a Resistance vehicle and driven away. After this, the regime gave up the mobilisation scheme as a total defeat, and the Reichskommissar instructed the press to remain quite silent about the whole affair.

To the Resistance leadership, the fight against labour mobilisation was a signal victory and a welcome encouragement after the difficulties of the previous year.

THE FINAL YEAR

Milorg: Sabotage and protection

The Allied invasion of Normandy on 6 June 1944 marked the beginning of the end for Hitler's Germany. From now on it was only a question of time. For the Norwegian Resistance, the invasion of the Continent had another significance, embodied in the so-called "June Directive" from Eisenhower's headquarters to the Norwegian Home Forces. In the changed strategic circumstances which had now arisen, the Directive began by stating: "No Allied military offensive operations are planned for this theatre, therefore no steps must be taken to encourage the Resistance Movement as such to overt action, since no outside support can be forthcoming." Norwegian Resistance was therefore to conserve its strength and avoid creating commitments to which the Allied armies could not respond.

At this time, the Allied Supreme Headquarters saw two possible developments in Norway: German collapse or surrender throughout, or a partial or complete German evacuation of Norwegian territory. For any of these alternatives, the main task of the Norwegian Resistance would be to protect essential installations such as power stations, communications and public utilities against a possible German "scorched earth" action.

The importance of these tasks was to be cruelly demonstrated later that year, when the German forces systematically destroyed the county of Finnmark in the north as they retreated before the advancing Russian troops on the Arctic front. With no Home Forces in the area and therefore no organised Resistance, the German forces had a free hand to evacuate the population, burn all the houses and blow up roads, boats, port installations and other constructions which could possibly have been of use to Germany's enemies.

In addition to their protection duties, the Home Forces would also have a crucial role to play in maintaining law and order until regular forces could enter the country. For the meantime, only certain sabotage actions against targets such as shipping, fuel and oil stores, and industrial plants of particular importance to the German war effort, could be carried out.

Although this directive meant severe limits on the natural desire of the Home Forces to prove themselves in action, the new tasks were no less demanding, and rather more constructive. The planning of these protective measures had long since been taken in hand by SOE and the Norwegian High Command in London, and could now be intensified after the amalgamation of SOE Norwegian Section and the fourth bureau of the Norwegian High Command, and the establishment, together with a Norwegian section of the American Office of Strategic Services, of a more unified command structure by way of a Special Force Headquarters. Along with the planning went an extensive build-up of the Home Forces to enable them to carry out their tasks efficiently. Scores of instructors were sent in during this last year, and arms, ammunition and equipment were supplied by submarine chasers from Shetland to the west coast, by air drops to the interior (213 drop operations for 1944 alone), or across the border from Sweden. Regular radio communications between the Home Forces and Britain were assured by a number of additional radio stations, with the result that in the final phase London had radio contact with all districts daily. Soon regular Home Force military bases were established in the mountains where whole units could receive systematic training and where arms and equipment could be received and stored. The first one, "Elg", was established in central South Norway in October 1944, followed by "Bjørn West" north of Bergen and, in the spring of 1945, "Varg" in the mountains north of Kristiansand. In this way the military

Milorg training for winter warfare.

Resistance approached the aim of a veritable secret army of thousands of well armed and trained men.

The importance of a Norwegian secret army would in any event be considerable during the liberation, since the physical transfer of Allied troops was bound to take some time. Its importance increased, however, as time passed and the Allied forces available for any "rescue operation" for Norway began to dwindle away. The stiff resistance met by the invasion armies on the Continent meant that all available reserves had to be put into action, and during the autumn of 1944 a British division that was intended as the mainstay of the liberation army for Norway had to be sent to the front. The Allied Commander for Norway had therefore to rely increasingly on the Norwegian forces in Britain and Sweden and on the Home Forces in order to prevent chaos in Norway.

In these circumstances, unity on the Home Front, and organisation and strict discipline in the Home Forces, were vitally necessary. The last winter was to provide evidence on both these counts. At the end of 1944, a unified and coordinated leadership of all Resistance organisations was constituted, including the "Circle", the Coordination Committee, the central leadership of the Home Forces, the underground police leadership and a committee on economic affairs. The expression "Hjemmefrontens Ledelse"—Leadership of the Home Front— had been used before, but from now on it meant one specific secret body of men with an undisputed leader: Chief Justice of the Supreme Court Paal Berg. Also, from December the Home Forces were able to demonstrate their capacity to act in accordance with a nation-wide plan.

The limited sabotage against specific aims, sanctioned by the Allied Supreme Headquarters, resulted in several spectacular actions during the autumn of 1944, particularly in the Oslo region. Specialists trained in Britain, cooperating with action groups from the Home Forces, thus succeeded on 14 August in blowing up a storage hall containing fuselages and engines for German fighter aircraft. A few days later a group from the Home Forces south-east of Oslo destroyed oil tanks with thousands of tons of submarine fuel. During September a destroyer was sunk at the Horten Naval Yard just as it was being made ready for active service in the German Navy, and a factory making anti-aircraft guns at Kongsberg was blown up. Then, in November, came the successful action in Oslo harbour by a communist-led group, which sank or heavily damaged about 50,000 tons of shipping. They also put out of action the only loading crane in the country capable of handling heavy tanks and artillery pieces. Through the autumn the leaders of the Home Forces continued to press for permission to attack a wider range of targets; in particular they urged a widespread attack on the railways. This would delay the withdrawal of German forces from Norway for use against the Allied advance on the Continent, and such actions were also necessary to give

The most successful railway sabotage: Jörstad bridge north of Trondheim in January 1945.

the Home Forces valuable experience and to prevent them from becoming demoralised through too much passivity.

The Allied commanders held back, until the Germans in the beginning of December 1944 counter-attacked in the Ardennes. The initial strength of the German thrust made it desirable to delay German troop movements from Norway, where they still had close to half a million soldiers, to the defence of Germany. Hence, the new Allied directive to the Home Forces, while emphasising the protection of vital installations as the primary task, opened the way to sabotage actions against railways with the aim of forcing the German troops to rely on sea transport—thus exposing them to Allied air and naval attack.

Preparations for railway sabotage were well in hand before this new directive was issued, and during December 1944 and

January 1945 nearly thirty sabotage attacks were carried out. Many created only minor damage and interrupted traffic for only a few days or even hours; but north of Trondheim an action group sent in from abroad blew up an important railway bridge on the only north-south connection in the area, causing the complete destruction of a German military train and blocking traffic for two weeks. Then, on the night of 14 March 1945 operation "Concrete Mixer" was launched: a concerted attack on a great number of railway lines, junctions, signal boxes and wagons all over the country, carried out by a total of more than a thousand saboteurs. While it is difficult to assess the exact results of the operation in terms of delays in German troop movements, the Home Forces had convincingly proved their ability to act in concert on a large scale, while preserving their readiness to strike again at short notice.

Civilian Resistance: Preparing for Peace

If the tasks for the civilian side of Resistance, as the end of the war approached, appeared less dramatic, the multitude and size of the problems to be faced was nevertheless immense. From early on it had been clear that when the war was over, it was no use thinking that Norway could just tear out the pages of its history covering the war, file them in the historian's archives, and resume on the basis of *status quo* as of March 1940. Some of the problems were obvious: vast numbers of German soldiers would have to be dealt with, and the several thousand inmates of German prison camps, imported for forced labour on military construction sites, would have to be taken care of and repatriated. For these tasks, Allied assistance would presumably be forthcoming, just as aid from abroad, prepared by the Government in London together with the Allies, would be needed to provide supplies of food and reconstruction materials and other kinds of help.

However, a complicated modern democratic nation does not function like a machine with a minimum of human attention. After a break of five years, normal political and administrative processes could not be re-started at the press of a button. To

80

begin from the top, the question of the postwar government until regular elections could be held could not be solved simply by the return of the exiled Ministers. Their relationship to the people under occupation had inevitably changed, and the Home Front leaders to whom the people were looking for guidance could not simply vanish into thin air, even if they wanted to, on the day of the liberation. And what about the Storting? Its role in the negotiations with the Germans in the summer of 1940 had not been a glorious one, and its authority was based on the elections of 1936, which now seemed a hundred years ago.

Similar problems arose at the local government level. Most prewar county governors, town mayors and councillors had been dismissed by the occupation regime, but even then not all of them had conducted themselves during the occupation in such a way as to earn the public confidence needed during the difficult transition to normalcy. Often new men would have to be found, and their functions would have to be regulated; but by whom: the Government abroad, or the Resistance leadership at home? And by what principles should they be selected and their powers defined: on the democratic basis for which the war had been fought,or with primary regard for authority and efficiency given the extraordinary circumstances?

Last, but not least, the war criminals, traitors and other collaborators would have to be dealt with in an efficient but orderly and just fashion. Popular sentiment after five years of repression was not inclined to tolerate any excessive leniency in the settlement with the collaborators. But it was essential to Norway's tradition of democratic justice that the due processes of law should be observed and that no "night of the long knives" should be allowed to blemish the record of Norwegian post-war democracy.

Such were the problems to which the Government in London and the civilian Resistance leaders turned their attention as the liberation approached. There were some disagreements, and often prolonged debates by secret courier mail, later supplemented by occasional conferences on neutral soil in Sweden, or even in London. But slowly a complete blueprint for the transition from war to peace evolved. A powerful influence towards agreement between the Government and the Home Front was the possibility that the Allied liberation armies, fearing a disunity among Norwegians that might threaten an orderly take-over from the German occupation, would impose an Allied military government on the country, thus replacing one occupation by another, however different. This would clearly be intolerable, and the way to avoid it was to show a united nation fully capable of taking over the management of the country without outside interference. This was also the basis for the agreements signed between the Norwegian Government and the Soviet, American and British Governments on 16 May 1944, regulating the jurisdiction and powers of the Allied military authorities which were to participate in the liberation. It must not be forgotten that, although Norway was primarily a British and secondarily an American responsibility, the first Allied soldiers to set foot on Norwegian soil as liberators were Russian. After Finland left the war in September 1944, and the Germans began their withdrawal from the Arctic regions, units of the Red Army pursued the enemy into the extreme north-east parts of Norway, thus liberating these provinces half a year before the rest of the country became free.

THE LIBERATION

As the end of the Third Reich approached, it was time to start the final preparations for the liberation of Norway, and the Resistance movement as well as the Norwegian and Allied authorities abroad were now getting ready for the last phase. In the last winter of the war, uncertainty as to how the war would end in Norway was widespread, and, by early spring of 1945, to believe in a peaceful take-over by the Norwegians seemed to be more than optimistic. The Norwegian Government and the Home Front leadership both feared that the German occupation might end in catastrophe for Norway. There were good reasons for this fear. As late as May 1945 the Germans still had about 350,000 Wehrmacht soldiers, well equipped and trained, in the fortified country. The Allies would have no troops to spare before Nazi Germany had been ultimately crushed—and what would happen in the meantime? Would the Nazis in Berlin flee to Festung Norwegen and make their last stand there? Or, even if the Wehrmacht in Germany capitulated, would the undefeated army in Norway follow suit? Knowledge of widespread German preparations to demolish bridges, roads, ports, hydro-electric stations and telephone exchanges, accompanied by reports of what had actually happened during German withdrawals in the north, underlined the seriousness of the situation. Moreover, even if the Wehrmacht in Norway accepted a general capitulation by the German High Command, what would Terboven and the SS do? And thousands of Norwegians were at the mercy of the Germans in prison camps all over the country.

Nothing could be done except prepare for the worst. To meet an increasing terror, or a situation where the lives of the Norwegian prisoners were endangered, the Home Front leadership worked out plans for a national strike. Also, the Norwegian Government tried to persuade the Swedes to mobilize and to stand ready to intervene, together with the Norwegian "police troops", in case the German army in Norway tried to prolong the war. A Swedish mobilization would exert additional pressure on the Germans by demonstrating the futility of a last stand in Norway. Norwegian "police troops" had been trained in Sweden, and by the spring of 1945 about 13,000 of them were ready as light infantry forces to play their part in the liberation of their country. Moreover, at the end of April the Allies on Eisenhower's request were preparing talks with Sweden to arrange for operations through Swedish territory against the German forces in Norway.

But much had to depend on Milorg. An approximate number of 40,000 Milorg men were the only armed forces actually on the spot. Milorg's main task was to protect Norwegian property and lives until help could arrive from abroad, and if the Wehrmacht in Norway chose not to surrender Milorg should support an Allied liberation force, which hopefully might be made available. The hope that the Wehrmacht leaders in Norway would see the futility of continued fight was however still

The order of the day from the Resistance Leadership: dignity, calmness, discipline!

there. Consequently the Norwegian authorities wanted neither to irritate nor to scare them by provocative actions of any kind. Norway would have everything to lose in an open fight with an enemy that had about ten fully trained and equipped soldiers to every Milorg man. The instruction to the nation, including Milorg, during the last weeks of the occupation was therefore quite simply: keep quiet, show discipline—and wait!

To the Norwegians at home and abroad the strain of waiting was nearly unbearable during the last days of the war. All over occupied Norway people gathered around "illegal" radios to follow the end of World War II: Hitler's suicide on 30 April; the surrender of the German forces in the Netherlands, northwestern Germany and Denmark on 5 May; and the unconditional surrender on all fronts declared by Dönitz, Hitler's successor, on 7 May. This included Norway, but would the German Commander-in-Chief in Norway, General Böhme, obey his orders?

It must have been a bitter decision to take. As he himself

84

said, the Germans in Norway were "undefeated and in posses-
sion of their full strength". On 7 May he had given the troops
orders to be on their guard and keep their formations, but *not*
to start any demolitions. Although he still hoped for better
conditions for his army than the unconditional surrender on
all the other fronts, he finally accepted the defeat. Through
Milorg Eisenhower had sent directives to Böhme telling him
how to establish radio contact with SHAEF, Supreme Headquarters Allied Expeditionary Force. This had been done to
give Böhme an opportunity to capitulate, and he used this
connection to inform the Allies that he now awaited the
arrival of the announced military mission. But he waited until
the morning of 8 May to do so. In the meantime, the Home
Front leadership had been in contact with the German headquarters at Lillehammer concerning the role of Milorg. Would
the Wehrmacht accept the Home Forces when they now appeared on the scene, or would a peaceful capitulation be endangered
by German irritation over this "civilian army"? Through a
Wehrmacht officer, who considered it his duty to work for a
peaceful surrender, contact with Böhme was established already in the night of 7/8 May. After a dramatic series of telephone talks, the Wehrmacht was at last convinced that the
appearance of Milorg would only be a guarantee for law and
order, and that it meant no danger to the German troops.

In the afternoon of 8 May an Allied military "mission" landed at Oslo airport and created some confusion. Böhme immediately telegraphed SHAEF to ask who "the 8 officers and
2 generals" were. These officers were heartily welcomed by the
Norwegians—and then disappeared as suddenly as they had
come. The whole visit turned out to be a private trip by some
Allied officers and journalists, who had flown up from Denmark to see how things were going in Norway ... Finally, the
real Allied armistice commission under the British Brigadier
Hilton arrived with a handful of officers, the only Allied
"troops" in Norway at the time, and made contact with the
German headquarters. The capitulation that followed was
more peaceful than the most optimistic forecasts. The Wehrmacht forces were told to withdraw from all fortifications and

The celebration begins.

assemble in certain areas, and to hand in their arms. The German discipline did not fail: in a few days they had carried out their orders, although at the time no one could have forced them to do so.

Actually, there were hardly any incidents at all during the liberation of Norway. A few die-hard Nazis, German and Norwegian, committed suicide, Terboven among them. Other SS and Gestapo officers tried to pass for ordinary Wehrmacht soldiers, having changed their uniforms, but most of them were later identified for the Allied authorities by Norwegian denouncers, who now tried to save themselves by betraying their former comrades.

The gayest and greatest celebration that Norway has ever seen started already on 7 May. As the news about Dönitz' capitulation spread, Norwegian flags appeared everywhere, and the streets were crowded with jubilant people. But until the

Showing the flag—their own policeman.

legal Government could take over, the Resistance leadership had the responsibility for law and order. This had been confirmed by the Norwegian Government in an historic message to the Home Front leadership on 5 May: "In the case of German capitulation in Norway, the Home Front leadership is hereby authorised on behalf of the Government to take the necessary steps for the maintenance of order and the establishment of Norwegian administration, based on Norwegian laws and regulations, until members of the Government arrive in Oslo . . ."

A proclamation from the leadership to the nation was printed during the night of 7 May, which stated that Norway was once more a free country, but warned that the enemy still had weapons. It was therefore imperative that no provocation should take place, and that the people should show discipline in the midst of their celebrations.

In the days between 7 and 9 May Milorg mobilized and took over the protection of official buildings and other strategic points all over the country. There were no clashes with the

The Royal Family on the review stand. Behind King Haakon stands Jens Christian Hauge, leader of Milorg.

Germans, whom Milorg had strict instructions to avoid. Of course this army of 40,000 young Norwegians, mostly dressed in civilian clothes with only an armband as identification, was most heartily welcomed by the population. Supported by Milorg, the secretly appointed civil servants took over central and local administration on 9 May. This of course included the police. Free newspapers were printed, the gates of the prison camps were opened, and the arrest of collaborators and war criminals began. Norwegian forces from abroad, including the 13,000 "police troops" trained in Sweden, arrived to assist Milorg in the maintenance of order, and some Allied forces were sent in to supervise the disarming and repatriation of German troops.

The rest of May was one big celebration. On 13 May Crown Prince Olav, Commander-in-Chief of all Norwegian Forces, returned home with some members of the Norwegian Government. This marked the end of the transitory rule by the Home Front leadership, who in a proclamation to the nation on 14 May declared their work done. The climax of the celebrations was reached on 7 June 1945, when HM King Haakon VII set foot on Norwegian soil again. He was welcomed by a nation ecstatic with joy; after five long, tragic years, Norway was at last a free country again.

From now on the problems were to be dealt with by the legal Norwegian authorities—the story of Norwegian Resistance in the Second World War had come to an end. It had been a long and bitter fight, and, although the occupation regime in Norway was less severe than had been the case in many other occupied countries, the struggle had taken its toll. No one knows for certain the number of Norwegians arrested for political reasons during the war, but it seems to have been between 30,000 and 40,000. According to official sources, the Resistance lost 2,091 men and women during the five years of occupation: 366 were executed; 162 were killed in open fight with the Germans; 130 died in prison in Norway, many of them either as a result of torture or because they committed suicide. In the concentration camps in Germany 1,340 Norwegian political prisoners lost their lives, among them 610 Jews, and the escape route across the North Sea took 93 lives. In addition comes an unknown number whose health had been ruined for life because of torture or maltreatment in prison.

What then, was the role and historical importance of the Norwegian Resistance Movement?

Perhaps primarily this: that it forged and maintained to the end a national unity over and above party political and other divisions, in defence of common national and democratic values against the occupant and his ideology. It also provided this united front with a direction and with a sense of purpose, kept the nation's fighting spirit alive in dark times, and channelled people's energies into positive action with the liberation of Norway as the ultimate goal.

Norwegian Resistance did not "win the war". The final victory over the Axis came through the massive military effort of the Allied great powers—an effort in which Norway, including its military Resistance, could only play a minor part. But the Resistance Movement, together with Norway-in-exile, enabled Norway to play that limited part effectively; and in the transition from war to peace, the Resistance by its unity, discipline and strength ensured that no part of the struggle had been in vain, and that Norway's post-war future be built on firm foundations.

The Home Forces on parade with rucksacks and windcheaters, marching towards the Royal Palace.

INDEX
(Italics refer to illustrations)

Administrative Council, 9—11, 15, 38.
Anglo-Norwegian Collaboration Committee (ANCC), 50.

BBC, 13, 22, 27, 35.
Berg, Paal, Chief Justice, *39*, 78.
"Björn West" (Home Forces base), 76.
Bräuer, German envoy, 15.
Böhme, General, 84—85.

Church, Norwegian Lutheran, 23—24, 41, 44.
Churchill, Winston, 29, 47.
Circle, The (Kretsen), 38—39, 66, 78.
"Claymore" operation, 31.
Communist resistance groups, 68, 72, 78.
"Concrete Mixer" operation, 80.
Coordination Committee (KK), 28, 39, 78.
Council of Commissioner Ministers, 13, 18.

"Donau", transport ship, *63*.

Education, Ministry of Church and, 23; attempts to indoctrinate school children, 41—43, 44.
Eisenhower, 75, 83, 85.
"Elg" (Home Forces base), 76.

Falkenhorst, General, 15.
Farmers' Association, 26.
Fishermen's Association, 26.
Fosdalen, 54.
"Freshman" operation, 60.

Gestapo, 28, 31, 50, 51, 52, 53, 55, 86; arrests trade unionists, 34.
Goebbels, 51.
Glomfjord, 54.
Grini prison camp, *35*.

Hagelin, Commissioner Minister of the Interior, 13, 18, 28.
Hambro, President of the Storting, 11.
Hauge, Jens Christian, head of Milorg, 67, *88*.
Heavy water sabotage, 59—61.
High Command, Norwegian, 33, 50, 76.
Haakon VII, 9, 11, *12*, 16, 18, 22, 32, 33, 56, 70, proclamation to the people of Norway, 12—13; returns to liberated Norway, *88*, 89.
Hilton, Brigadier, 85.
Hitler, 11, 40, 46, 48, 58, 75, 84.
"Hjemmefrontens Ledelse" (Leadership of the Home Front), 78.
Home Forces, 76, 78, 80, 85, *91*.

"Jupiter" operation, 47, 53.
Jörstad Bridge, *79*, 80.

KK, see Coordination Committee.
Koht, Halvdan, Foreign Minister, 12.
Kretsen, see Circle.

Labour service, 71—72, 73—75.
Linge, Martin, leader of Norwegian Independent Company No. 1, 30.
Linge Company, 48—49, 52, 53—54, 60.
Lofoten raid, 40.
Lysaker Bridge, 15.

Majavatn, 53, 54.
Medical Association, 28.
Milorg (military organisation in Norway), 31—33, 48, 49—50, 62, *77*; hit by Gestapo, 52, 53; being reorganised, 55—56; debate on future role, 63—67, 69; tasks during liberation, 83—84, 85, 87.

Nasjonal Samling (Norwegian Nazi Party), 9, 13, 18—20, 23, 24, 26, 38, 39; and indoctrination in schools, 40—43; and the Church, 44.
National Youth Organisation, 41—43.
Norwegian Government in Exile, 9, 11, 18, 56, 59, 69, 87, 89; contacts with Resistance Movement, 22—23, 28—29, 32—33, 64; post-war problems, 80—82.
Norwegian Supreme Court, 10, 20—21, 38.

Olav, Crown Prince, 70, 88, 89.
Orkla mines, 61.
OSS, Office of Strategic Studies, 76.
Oslo University, 71.

Police, Norwegian, 72, 87.
Police troops, Norwegian, in Sweden, 83.

Quisling, Vidkun, 10, 13, 15, 18, 19, 22, 24, 25, 38, 41, 42, 74; declares himself Prime Minister, 9; installed as "Ministerpresident", 39—40; and the Church, 44; tries to establish "Riksting", 44—46; and the police, 72.

Red Army, 82.
Rediess, German Police General, 14, 41.
Riisnaes, S. P., Commissioner Minister of Justice, 20, 73.
"Riksting" plans, 40, 43, 44.
Rinnan Henry Oliver, Gestapo informer, 51, 53.
Rjukan, 59—60.

Sabotage, 15, 30, 31, 32, 48, 59—62, 67, 68, 72, 76, 78—80.
Scharffenberg, Johan, 16.
Shetland, 30, 32, 48, 51, 76.
SIS (Secret Intelligence Service), 47—48, 51.
SOE (Special Operations Executive), 22, 29—32, 47, 48, 51, 53, 59, 60, 61, 67, 76; begins to cooperative with Milorg, 49—50, 54—55.
Sports associations, 26—27.
Stalin, 47.
Stord mines, 61.
Storting (Norwegian Parliament), 11, 13, 81.

Teachers, 24, 41—43.
Telavåg, 51—52.
Terboven, Joseph, Reichskommissar, 9, 14, 16, 21, 27, 28, 33, 37, 39, 40, 41, 44, 46, 54, 71, 83, 86; sets up Council of Commissioner Ministers, 13; initiates wave of terror in Oslo, 34; and the teachers, 42.
"Tirpitz", German battleship, 48, 49.
"Total nation labour effort", see Labour service.
Trade unions, 28, 33, 44, 46.

Underground press, 35—37.

"Varg" (Home Forces base), 76.
Vågsöy raid, 40.